Going circular

Unlocking the potential of regions and cities to drive the circular economy transition

Edited by Marcin Dąbrowski, Karel Van den Berghe, Joanna Williams and Ellen van Bueren

Regional Studies Policy Impact Books
Series Editor: Louise Kempton

ROUTLEDGE
Routledge
Taylor & Francis Group
LONDON AND NEW YORK

RSA Regional Studies Association
Research Today, Policy Tomorrow

First published 2024
by Taylor & Francis
4 Park Square, Milton Park, Abingdon, Oxon, OX14 4RN

Taylor & Francis Group, an informa business

British Library Cataloguing-in-Publication Data
A catalogue record for this book is available from the British Library.

ISBN13: 978-1-041-00225-3 (print)
ISBN13: 978-1-003-60876-9 (e-book)

Typeset in 10.5/13.5 Myriad Pro
by Nova Techset Private Limited, Bengaluru and Chennai, India

Disclosure statement: No potential conflict of interest was reported by the authors.

The cover image and all infographics were produced by Fábio Alzate Martinez.

Please visit https://taylorandfrancis.com/about/corporate-responsibility/accessibility-at-taylor-francis/ for further information on the accessibility features available for Regional Studies Policy Impact Books

CONTENTS

Going circular

Unlocking the potential of regions and cities to drive the circular economy transition

About the editors 1

About the authors 3

Executive summary 5

1. Circular regions and cities: towards a spatial perspective on circular economy 13
Marcin Dąbrowski, Joanna Williams, Karel Van den Berghe and Ellen Van Bueren

1.1 Overview 15
1.2 Introduction 15
1.3 The elusive definition of circular economy 16
1.4 Why do cities and regions matter? 17
1.5 Circular policies in want of a spatial dimension 19
1.6 Defining a circular city and a circular region 20
1.7 Knowledge and policy gaps 22
1.8 Conclusions 23

2. The window of opportunity for circular economy in Europe in the wake of the geopolitical turmoil: connecting scales and principles 29
Karel Van den Berghe and Marcin Dąbrowski

2.1 Overview 31
2.2 We are at war(s)! 31
2.3 Fortress circular economy: from a negative to a positive narrative? 33
2.4 Scales of circular economy applications 34
2.5 Localism as a result of the geopolitical turmoil 36
2.6 The localism principle of circular economy is the most important one 37
2.7 Conclusions 39

3. Towards a care-full circular economy 43
Federica Bono, Wendy Wuyts and Elmar Willems

3.1 Overview 45
3.2 Introduction 45

3.3 Care-less reuse, repair and recycling practices 47
3.4 Examples of care-full circular economy 49
3.5 Key learning points for policy 52
3.6 Conclusions 54

4. Implementing the circular bioeconomy in metropolitan regions **61**
Joanna Williams

4.1 Overview 63
4.2 Introduction 63
4.3 Brief overview of how the problem has been tackled in academic and policy research 64
4.4 Brief overview of how the problem has been tackled in practice 65
4.5 Challenges for circular bioeconomies in city-regions 68
4.6 Lack of institutional competencies and resources for metropolitan planning 68
4.7 The unequal distribution of dis/benefits 70
4.8 Synergies and conflicts with existing urban policies 70
4.9 Siloed thinking in policymaking leading to suboptimal strategies 71
4.10 Lack of data for metropolitan resource and ecosystem service management 71
4.11 Engaging local stakeholders in metro-planning 74
4.12 Conclusions 74

5. Assessing circular economy transitions **81**
Marcin Dąbrowski and Alexander Wandl

5.1 Overview 83
5.2 The challenge of assessing the state of circular economy transitions 83
5.3 Insights from research 84
5.4 State of play in policy practice 87
5.5 Conclusions: principles for an integrated and place-based circular economy assessment 92

6. Policy recommendations for facilitating an urban and regional circular economy **99**
Karel Van den Berghe, Marcin Dąbrowski, Ellen Van Bueren and Joanna Williams

6.1 Overview 101
6.2 The main messages of this book 101
6.3 Policy recommendations 102
7 In closing 107

About the editors

Marcin Dąbrowski teaches and researches spatial planning and (multi-level) governance issues related to sustainable urban and regional futures. He is based at the Department of Urbanism, Delft University of Technology, the Netherlands. With a background in political science and experience in research on spatial planning systems, diverse territorial policies and participatory practices, Marcin operates as a boundary-spanner creating bridges across disciplines, academic "tribes" and societal groups. Marcin has published extensively on Europeanisation of regional and urban policies, the governance of the European Union's Cohesion Policy and policy transfer. His more recent work explores questions of governance, policy learning and citizen participation in the context of sustainability transitions in cities and regions. This includes topics such as integration of flood risk management with spatial planning, stakeholder engagement in water-linked heritage valorisation (Interreg WaVE), the socio-spatial dimensions of the circular economy (H2020 REPAiR project), participatory carbon-neutrality experimentation in cities (HE UP2030 project), cross-fertilisation between Cohesion Policy and spatial planning across diverse European contexts (ESPON COMPASS), and engagement of marginalised communities in just-sustainability transitions in regions heavily dependent on energy-intensive industries (HE DUST project). Marcin is a member of the board of the Regional Studies Association, with the territorial networks portfolio.
m.m.dabrowski@tudelft.nl https://orcid.org/0000-0001-6775-0664

Karel Van den Berghe is Assistant Professor in Spatial Planning and Urban Development Management at the Department of Management in the Built Environment, Delft University of Technology, the Netherlands. He holds a master's in geography as well as a master's in spatial planning and urbanism. His doctorate focused on the relational port–city interface, exploring how the socio-economic planning of urban and maritime systems should co-op with ongoing transitions. More recently, Karel has focused on the question of the role of space in the circular economy (Circular Campus project), the increasing geopolitical turmoil due to re-/de-globalisation (NWO KIC SUBLIME project and NTNU 1-2-Tre-Steg project), the use of a scenario methodology for uncertain spatial planning (South Holland urban water-bound industrial areas project and NWA-ORC Accelerating the Circular Transition), and the importance of industrial functions in or nearby urban knowledge areas as an answer, first, to localising global production networks and, second, to a beautiful and inclusive urban planning (HE FABRIX project). Karel is a member of the steering committee of the TU Delft Faculty of Architecture and Built Environment Circular Built Environment Hub, advisor to the Dutch Council for Infrastructure and Environment, and a member of the advisory board of the Dutch Knowledge Alliance Industrial and Business Areas. He often advises port authorities, municipalities, provinces, the Dutch and Flemish governments, and the European Commission. Karel is a Regional Studies Association Fellow 2023 (FeRSA). K.B.J.VandenBerghe@TUDelft.nl https://orcid.org/0000-0001-8395-0586

Joanna Williams is Director of the Circular Cities Hub and Professor in Sustainable Development at the Bartlett School of Planning, UCL, London, UK. She is also Visiting Professor at TU Delft, the Netherlands. Jo has 26 years of research experience, writing on a range of topics focused on reducing resource consumption and human-induced greenhouse gas emissions in urban and regional systems. She works closely with consultants, industry, government and cities. She advises international bodies – European Commission, European Environment Agency, Organisation for Economic Co-operation and Development (OECD) and UN-Habitat — on the delivery of regenerative, circular, resilient, low-carbon urban systems; sustainable consumption and production; and sustainable urban transitions. Jo has had several large European and international research projects focused on these topics. She set up the Circular Cities Hub Network in 2016 to enable the exchange of knowledge between academia, policymakers and practitioners on implementing circular urban systems. She has published widely, including *Zero Carbon Homes: A Road Map* (2011) and *Circular Cities: A Revolution in Urban Sustainability* (2021) (both Routledge). She was recently commended for the Royal Town Planning Institute's (RTPI) Peter Hall award for research excellence for her research on circular cities.
Joanna.williams@ucl.ac.uk https://orcid.org/0000-0003-0377-8654

Ellen van Bueren is Professor of Urban Development Management and head of the Department of Management in the Built Environment, Delft University of Technology, the Netherlands. The governance of sustainable urban areas is at the core of Ellen's research and teaching. With a background in urban planning and public policy, she analyses and advises on decision-making in complex, multi-actor settings, public and private, including questions of governance, organisation and regulation. As a Professor of Urban Development Management she further develops a generalised, theoretical understanding of processes of urban development and the management thereof, which can be of use to stakeholders involved in urban development projects. Ellen has published on topics such as institutional barriers for sustainable construction, the mainstreaming of green building, sustainable urban development, renewable energy policy and implementation, and evaluation of environmental policy. She has edited *Sustainable Urban Environments: An Ecosystem Approach* (Springer, 2012). Together with Bertien Broekhans, Ellen wrote a chapter on mainstreaming niche innovations for Rebecca Henn and Andrew Hoffman's book *Constructing Green - The Social Structures of Sustainability* (MIT Press, 2013), that received an Honorable Mention at the 2014 Best Book Award from the Organizations & Natural Environment Division of the Academy of Management.
e.m.vanbueren@tudelft.nl https://orcid.org/0000-0002-4375-1192

About the authors

Federica Bono is Assistant Professor of Human Geography at Christopher Newport University (CNU), Newport News, Virginia, USA. Before joining CNU, she was a lecturer at Old Dominion University, Norfolk, Virginia. She holds a doctorate in geography from the University of Leuven (KUL), Belgium, an MSc in geography from KUL and an MSc in urban and regional planning from the University of Birmingham, UK. Her doctoral dissertation – funded by Fonds voor Wetenschappelijk Onderzoek (FWO) Vlaanderen – investigated Cuba's diverse informal and solidary food economy. Her most recent work investigates informal and solidarity relations in the first food economy in Hampton Roads, Virginia, and lies at the intersection of the geography of food, feminist political economy and critical legal geography. In addition to fieldwork in Cuba, she has conducted fieldwork in Belgium, Spain, Gibraltar, the UK and the United States. She has written and published about food access, (cross-border) solidarity relations, alternative and informal food economies, and care in early-career academia. At CNU, she teaches human geography and geographical information system (GIS) courses, created the GIS and cartography curriculum, and co-created the geography minor. From 2025 she will be Assistant Professor of Human Geography at the University of Amsterdam. federica.bono@cnu.edu
https://orcid.org/0000-0002-2617-9091

Alexander Wandl is Associate Professor and head of the Section of Environmental Technology and Design of the Department of Urbanism, Faculty of Architecture and the Built Environment, Delft University of Technology, the Netherlands. He is a steering committee member of the Circular Built Environment Hub, TU Delft's Think Tank for the circularity transition from the material scale to the region. Alex uses an extended territorial metabolism approach, integrating methods and tools from urban planning and design, landscape architecture, and spatial data science in a multiscale approach to sustainable urbanism. In the last years, his research and teaching has focused on the spatial dimension of the circularity transitions of cities and regions. He specifically concentrated on the challenges related to the sustainable development of dispersed urban areas and peri-urbanisation processes in Europe. As scientific coordinator of the Horizon 2020 financed research project REPAiR – Resource Management in Peri-Urban Areas — he steered the development of place and activity-based flow and stock mapping methods that were used in spatial plans across Europe, most prominently in the Amsterdam Circular Monitor. Alex developed interdisciplinary online, and on-campus education at the master's and professional levels to educate future circular economy advocates on integrating circularity strategies into regional planning and design. a.wandl@tudelft.nl
https://orcid.org/0000-0003-1163-0529

Elmar Willems is Program Lead Circular Local Governance at Circular Flanders, the hub for the circular economy transition in Flanders, Belgium. As a longstanding policy-officer at the Public Flemish Waste Agency, the regional authority for waste management and soil policies, Elmar has been closely engaged with issues of resource management, policy innovation and project development for a circular economy. His focus lies with circular cities, circular area development and brownfields. He holds a master's degree in environmental policy sciences from Radboud University, Nijmegen, the Netherlands. He is co-author of *Lokaal en Circulair, werken aan de toekomst* (Local and Circular, Crafting the Future) (Politeia, 2020), and guest editor of the magazine *RUIMTE* (Space). elmar.willems@ovam.be

Wendy Wuyts, with a doctorate from Nagoya University, Japan, has contributed to the discourse on the social circular economy approach to the built environment. Focusing on the role of data in achieving circularity in urban structures, her part-time work with the Norwegian start-up Omtre delves into digital circularity in the timber built environment (e.g., HEU DRASTIC project, Green Platform projects SirkTRE and CircWOOD). Wendy remains committed to her independent research endeavour to support just circular cities that advocate for multispecies inclusion, embrace biocultural heritage and recognise the invisible. Her collaboration with Circular Flanders resulted in projects such as Bold Branders, which combined storytelling with circular economy principles and culminated in experimental events and an eco-fiction novel, and C-Power, an initiative that introduced young individuals, especially those from challenging backgrounds, to the tenets of circular economy in two Flemish cities. Wendy has conducted extensive research across multiple countries, such as Japan, Thailand, the United States, Mexico, Norway and Svalbard, the Netherlands and Belgium. Additionally, she regularly contributes to the Belgian magazine *Mo**, discussing circular economy topics, collaborates with government officers across Europe on resources' governance for circular cities, and organises nature-based restor(y)ing events. wendywwuyts@gmail.com
https://orcid.org/0000-0002-7383-2428

 https://doi.org/10.1080/2578711X.2024.2418239

Executive Summary

This book explores the concept of a circular economy (CE) and its transformative potential for cities and regions. It emphasises the importance of spatial planning and the role of urban and regional authorities in driving the transition to a more sustainable, resilient, and inclusive economic and societal model. As such, the book aims to inform and equip public and private policymakers, urban planners and regional authorities with the knowledge and tools needed to foster a CE, and nudge cities and regions towards sustainable futures.

Urbanised regions face mounting challenges related to environmental degradation, resource scarcity, social inequality and economic instability. Instead of "take–make–waste", CE aims to reduce waste, reuse resources and regenerate natural systems, while fostering resilience and inclusivity. This book offers a fresh perspective on CE by stressing its spatial dimensions and the critical role of cities and regions as pivotal actors in the transition to a circular future. At the same time, it offers a critical perspective on this topic and stresses that there is no one-size-fits-all approach to regional and urban CE policies. Instead, it advocates a context-specific understanding of CE, emphasising the importance of local and regional conditions for circular activities, of the spatial patterns in resource stocks and flows within territories, and of the need to engage a range of stakeholders and communities in decision-making processes.

The book's objectives are as follows:

- To draw attention to the spatial dimensions of CE and how they influence the implementation of CE policies.
- To explore the opportunities provided by current geopolitical shifts to advance CE.
- To integrate social justice and care into the CE framework.
- To explore the ecological implications of a transition towards CE in metropolitan regions.
- To advocate the need for robust metrics for assessing the progress on the transition towards CE.
- To formulate policy recommendations for various levels of government to promote CE.

https://doi.org/10.1080/2578711X.2024.2418237

Reflecting these objectives, the book's six chapters tackle the pivotal policy issues and challenges related CE transitions in cities and regions.

1 TOWARDS A SPATIAL PERSPECTIVE ON CIRCULAR ECONOMY

The opening chapter stresses that the transition to CE must consider the spatial dimensions and unique characteristics of cities and regions. Effective CE policies should be tailored to specific urban and regional contexts, recognising that the implementation of these policies occurs within distinct spatial settings. Current approaches to CE policies tend lack such a spatial perspective. Policymakers should prioritise place-based strategies that leverage local resources, infrastructure and community strengths to create sustainable, circular systems.

A circular city is defined as a complex, regenerative and adaptive socio-ecological system consisting of a bio-geophysical unit and its associated social actors and institutions. It pursues three types of circular actions: looping actions (recycling, reusing and energy recovery), ecologically regenerative actions (restoring ecosystems and ecosystem services) and adaptive actions (flexible design and planning, co-creating, and learning environments); whereas a circular region is a system of interdependencies and connections created by material flows between the different types of territories (urban, industrial, peri-urban and rural), nature and the built environment, actors and networks. The goal is to nurture regenerative natural cycles supported by adapted socio-technological and socio-ecological systems, structuring looped systems of materials and energy within the regional space.

The five principles of a CE — circular flow of materials and energy, slowing down these flows, reducing the amount of materials and energy used, substituting non-sustainable materials with sustainable ones, and prioritising local circulation of materials and products — should guide this transition. By understanding the spatial interdependencies and implications of "going circular" within regions, policymakers and planners can design CE strategies that enhance local economies, regenerate degraded areas, and improve regional resilience. Integrating CE principles in spatial planning can maximise the benefits of circular activities, ensuring alignment with broader goals of sustainability.

2 THE GEOPOLITICAL WINDOW OF OPPORTUNITY FOR THE CIRCULAR ECONOMY

The second chapter puts forward the argument that the convergence of climate change and geopolitical conflicts presents a unique window of opportunity to advance CE, especially in the European context. Current geopolitical turmoil, particularly the war in Ukraine, has highlighted the vulnerabilities of relying on external resources and the need for local resilience. This situation emphasises the importance of the fifth CE principle — localism — which involves developing as-local-as-possible production and consumption systems to enhance sustainability and reduce dependencies on global value chains.

Such a local perspective on CE calls for the integration of economic activities within specific geographical areas to better meet local needs and responsibilities. This principle is crucial because it clarifies who is responsible for CE actions (the municipality, the regional authority and all the relevant related actors) and ensures that both the benefits and burdens of these actions are appropriately distributed. The current geopolitical context provides a momentum to operationalise this principle, linking it to territorial policies and development strategies.

However, implementing CE at local and regional levels is not without its challenges. There is, for example, a potential spatial conflict between the industrial (re)manufacturing or waste-processing activities and residential functions. In many cases, waste management and other burdensome activities have been externalised beyond urban areas to the hinterland and peripheral areas. Now there is a need to rethink spatial strategies to internalise these functions within cities and regions, ensuring that the local benefits of CE are maximised while mitigating any adverse impacts, such as increased traffic related to logistics, odour or noise.

A key recommendation for policymakers from this chapter is to seize this geopolitical moment to drive CE by integrating the localism principle into spatial planning and regional development policies. This involves designing and implementing circular policies that not only focus on economic and technological aspects but also consider social and ecological dimensions in spatial policymaking. Policymakers should foster collaborations across different levels of government and sectors to ensure that CE principles are effectively embedded in urban and regional planning frameworks.

By capitalising on this window of opportunity, Europe could move towards a more resilient and sustainable future. This transition requires a coordinated effort to develop and implement CE strategies that are adaptive, inclusive and responsive to both local and global challenges.

3 CARE-FULL CIRCULAR ECONOMY

Traditional approaches to CE often emphasise technocentric and profit-driven models, which can overlook critical social and environmental dimensions. The third chapter advocates a "care-full" CE that integrates care and social justice into policy frameworks, challenging the prevailing focus on economic and technological indicators. This approach prioritises human and non-human relationships and dependencies, recognising that sustainability requires attention to social equity, inclusivity and ecological integrity.

Policymakers should adopt a care-full approach by emphasising five key dimensions:

1) *Care for Carers:* Recognise and value the contributions of those who perform the essential work of maintaining circular systems, ensuring fair compensation and support across socio-economic and geographical lines.

2) *Care for Materials:* Move beyond technocratic views of materials to appreciate their social and ecological contexts, drawing inspiration from indigenous and informal practices that embody principles of solidarity and justice.

3) *Care for Space:* Ensure communal access to non-market spaces that foster social–circular innovation and experimentation, linking these spaces with well-being indicators such as identity and heritage preservation.

4) *Care for Time:* Re-evaluate project timelines to embrace "slowness", which allows for the long-term political and caring work necessary for a sustainable transition and optimises the scheduling of public services to reduce travel distances and times.

5) *Care for Difference:* Build inclusive communities by valuing the diverse practices and experiences of local actors, moving from damage- to desire-centred approaches that recognise and empower marginalised groups.

By integrating these care principles, CE policies for cities and regions can become more ecologically sustainable and socially just. This shift requires policymakers to rethink CE strategies, focusing not only on economic efficiency but also on fostering high-quality social and ecological relationships.

4 CIRCULAR BIOECONOMY IN METROPOLITAN REGIONS

Adopting a regenerative circular approach to (re)development in metropolitan regions is crucial for reducing urban ecological footprints and enhancing resource security, as is argued in the fourth chapter. This approach emphasises the interconnectedness of urban areas and their surrounding ecosystems, advocating for policies that foster urban circular bioeconomies by regenerating natural systems and promoting local resource production. Current CE policies often focus narrowly on recycling and reusing materials, overlooking the broader ecological impacts and the need for healthy urban ecosystems.

To foster circular bioeconomies in metropolitan regions, policymakers must consider the intrinsic link between cities and their hinterlands. This involves planning for resource resilience by ensuring that urban areas not only consume resources but also contribute to their regeneration. Key strategies include enhancing local food, water and energy production, and developing infrastructure that supports ecological health. CE policies should incorporate land, soil, vegetation, clean air and water as critical resources, ensuring that urban ecosystems are maintained and restored.

Implementing these strategies requires a shift from linear to systems thinking in policy frameworks. This means moving away from siloed approaches and fostering collaboration across sectors and administrative boundaries. Metropolitan institutions need to develop capacities for strategic planning and resource management, leveraging cross-boundary coordination to optimise resource flows and the provision of ecosystem services.

Policymakers are encouraged to prioritise ecological goals in circular development frameworks, tailoring strategies to the specific bioregional and cultural contexts of metropolitan areas. This includes creating metropolitan plans that synergise resource looping, regenerative and adaptive strategies, while engaging local stakeholders in the planning and implementation processes. Evidence-based decision-making tools that map resource flows and ecosystem services are essential for informed policymaking and community engagement.

By adopting an approach promoting an urban circular bioeconomy, metropolitan regions can reduce their ecological footprints, enhance resource security, and improve the overall health and resilience of urban ecosystems. This transition requires a collaborative effort and innovative policy instruments that support the integration of ecological, social and economic goals.

5 ASSESSING CIRCULAR ECONOMY TRANSITIONS

Accurately assessing the transition towards a CE is critical for informing policy and guiding effective implementation in cities and regions, as is argued in the fifth chapter. Current assessment methods often lack integration of the relevant dimensions and adequate data, particularly regarding spatial governance and social aspects of CE transitions. Policymakers need to develop robust tools to monitor progress, evaluate impacts and identify areas for improvement.

To support CE transitions, it is essential to measure the impacts of circular activities in terms not only of material stocks and flows but also of governance performance, citizen awareness and behavioural changes. Existing frameworks often focus narrowly on waste management and resource efficiency, missing broader social and spatial impacts that circular actions may have.

Effective assessment frameworks should consider environmental, social and economic impacts of material looping processes, addressing potential negative effects in terms of sustainability such as high energy use in recycling or increased emissions from transportation. Aligning life cycle assessment (LCA) with the United Nations' Sustainable Development Goals (SDGs) can provide a more comprehensive evaluation of CE activities, highlighting their interconnectedness with broader sustainability objectives.

Figure 1 Overview of the policy recommendations

SCALE	RECOMMENDATIONS
International 	1 - Promote the development of standardised approaches to collecting data on waste, material flows and stocks at the national and regional levels 2 - Embrace an integral approach to evaluating the impacts of circular economy initiatives 3 - Invest in research and development of new metrics to capture the social, environmental, economic and spatial dimensions and impacts of circular economy at different levels 4 - Invest in the development of capacity for steering and informing circular economy transitions
National 	1 - Set ambitious circular economy transition agendas and foster a cross-sectoral dialogue ato engage the big economic and societal players at the national scale 2 - Incentivise the adoption of circular principles by sub-national governments, companies and citizens through regulation, taxation, finance, and other policy tools 3 - Use circular economy as a strategic backbone for integration of goals and actions across the relevant national policies 4 - Develop national strategies to limit resource consumption 5 - Propose spatial visions and strategies that embrace circular economy as an important factor for national spatial development
Regional / Local 	1 - Nurture territorially-embedded communities of practice to inform policy and spatial planning for circular economy transition 2 - Use interregional or international ciruclar economy knowledge co-creation and sharing platforms to learn and draw lessons 3 - Embrace a 'care-full' approach to circular activities, using them as a vector for social justice and inclusion 4 - Rethink and valorise interconnections across urban, peri-urban, rural areas through the prism of material flows to harness the regenerative potential of circular economy 5 - Strengthen capacities, resources and competences of the regional authorities to provide a strong institutional leadership needed to bring regional stakeholders together to promote the circular economy agenda within the new functional geographies shaped by material flows

Source: Authors; graphic design by Fábio Alzate Martinez (TU Delft)

Finally, policymakers should also focus on enabling institutional environments to facilitate CE transitions. This involves assessing strategic-level activities, tactical transition actions, local experimentation and collective learning. Evaluating how the CE transition unfolds in the built environment is crucial, as CE activities are grounded in specific territories and infrastructures. Assessments should examine the implementation of circular construction methods, spatial re-organisation of economic activities and the suitability of urban planning regulations to support circular practices.

6 TOWARDS CIRCULAR CITIES AND REGIONS

The sixth and final chapter summarises the main policy lessons. To transition to CE effectively, policy actions must be coordinated across international, national and local scales (Figure 1). Each level of governance plays a specific role in promoting and implementing CE principles in regions and cities.

Marcin Dąbrowski, Karel Van den Berghe, Joanna Williams and Ellen Van Bueren

1. Circular regions and cities: towards a spatial perspective on circular economy

Marcin Dąbrowski, Joanna Williams, Karel Van den Berghe and
Ellen Van Bueren

Keywords: circular economy; regions; cities; space; spatial planning; policy

De Ceuvel, a 'city playground for innovation, experimentation and creativity' in Amsterdam. *Source*: Superbaas
https://commons.wikimedia.org/wiki/File:2019-06-09-De_Ceuvel-1.jpg

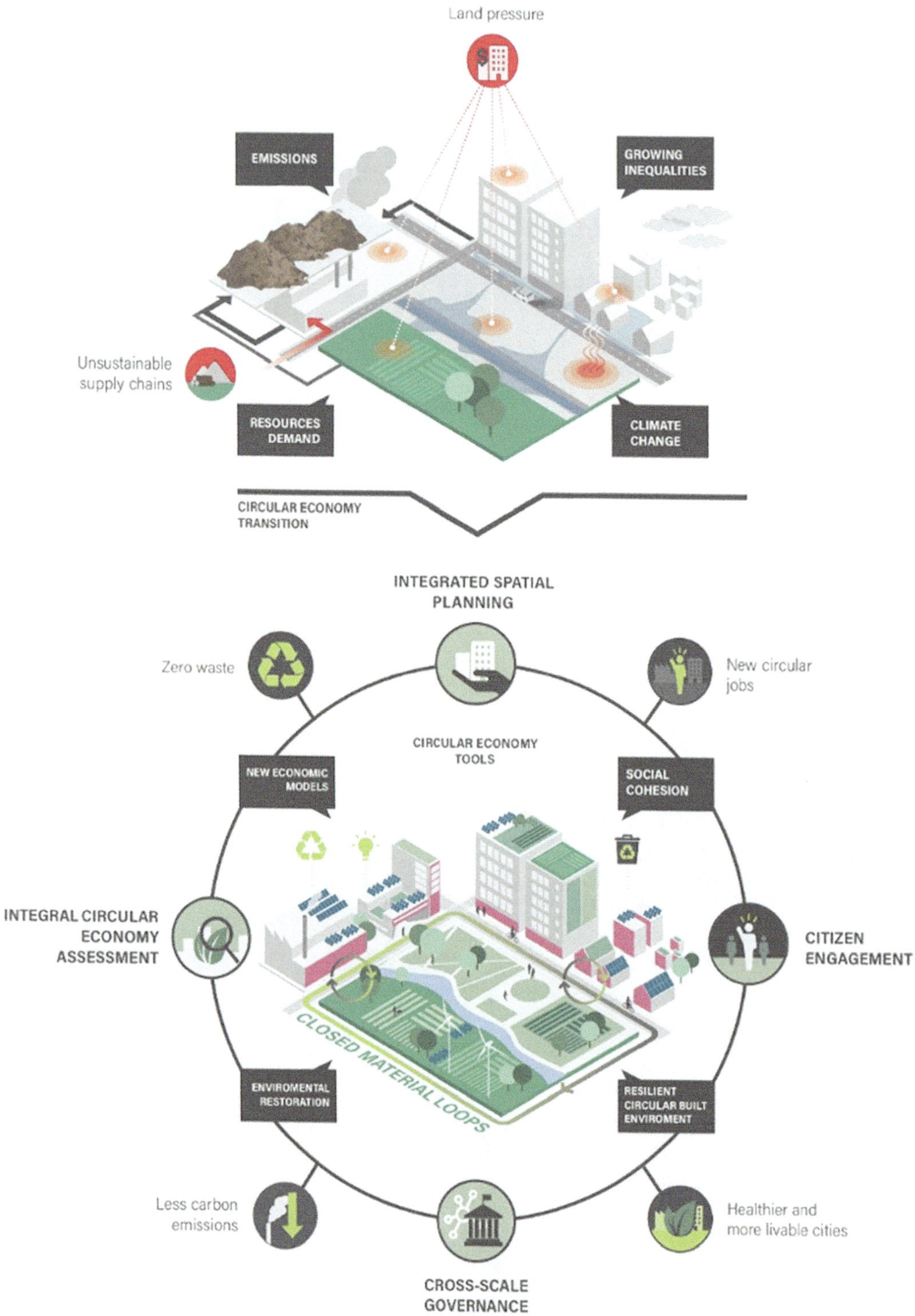

Source: Authors; graphic design by Fábio Alzate Martinez (TU Delft)

Key message

If a circular perspective is effectively integrated into spatial planning and territorial policies, we can generate numerous synergies from moving towards circular futures.

1.1 OVERVIEW

Circular economy (CE) is territorialised. Economic activities are spatially embedded; they operate across a variety of scales and are heavily influenced by their spatial context. Yet the CE academic literature and policy frameworks rarely address this dimension. If CE policies are to achieve sustainable development goals and be implementable at a subnational level, these shortcomings need to be addressed. In this chapter, we take stock of the current debates and policy on CE in cities and urban regions, critiquing them from a spatial, socio-ecological and governance perspective. On that basis, we outline a new policy and research agenda to bridge the above-mentioned gap and inform the development and implementation of place-based CE policies.

1.2 INTRODUCTION

Cities and their hinterlands are at the heart of several intertwined crises. The activities concentrated in cities are one of the main drivers of climate change, yet cities are also among the primary victims of its impacts (heatwaves, flooding). Urban regions are further impacted by biodiversity loss and environmental degradation, driven by industrial activity, real-estate development and the expansion of urban infrastructure. There is also a housing crisis, exacerbated by the financialisation of property markets and growing demand from expanding urban populations. Meanwhile, the negative impacts of the COVID-19 pandemic have disproportionately affected less affluent urban dwellers, making cities increasingly unaffordable. Finally, cities are also affected by the energy crises that emerged in the context of current geopolitical volatility. Cities consume 80% of the world's resources and produce 50% of the waste.[1] It is projected that between 2015 and 2030 large cities will account for 81% of resource consumption and 91% of consumption growth.[2] Meanwhile, cities already face resource scarcity issues, particularly with water, energy and food. At the same time, peri-urban areas and rural regions are increasingly affected by the negative externalities of urbanisation. These include, among others, land-grabbing to meet the high demand for space for housing and business activities, pollution and nuisance from waste management facilities, renewable energy production displacing farmers and damaging natural landscapes, and the increasingly industrialised and polluting agriculture required to cater to the growing number of city dwellers.

Given these overlapping crises and pressures, and the fact that addressing them would require far-reaching and possibly unpopular policy changes, there is an urgent need for new ideas and approaches to rethink urban and regional development. The CE concept, promoting the reduction of waste generation and resource consumption through symbiotic relations between economic activities in closed material loops, is increasingly brought up in this debate as a framework for rethinking the ways in which cities and regions can develop without overshooting the finite planetary boundaries that set the limits for economic growth.[3,4]

In this chapter, we take stock of the current debates and policy on CE in cities and regions, proposing a critique from a spatial, socio-geographical and governance perspective. On that basis, we outline a new agenda for regional and urban researchers, policymakers and practitioners to bridge the above-mentioned gaps, and inform the development and implementation of place-based CE policies.

1.3 THE ELUSIVE DEFINITION OF CIRCULAR ECONOMY

As with any new and popular concept, many definitions are put forward, resulting in some confusion.[5,6] While the concept emerged in the industrial ecology field, related to the notion of symbiosis between branches of industry where the waste of one can be used as a resource for another, and is still often associated with waste management, its use rapidly spread across many disciplines. The most widely used definition is probably that by the Ellen MacArthur Foundation (EMF),[7] which states that CE is "an industrial system that is restorative or regenerative by intention and design" and uses principles of circulation of products and materials (at their highest value), "designing out" waste and the regeneration of degraded ecosystems, as opposed to the current extractive approach to Earth's resources.

Others stress that CE is operationalised in systems at various levels,[8,9] from the micro-level (related to products, companies or consumer behaviour), through meso-level (related to industrial parks where symbiosis and material looping can take place) to macro-level (related to city, region, nation, etc.), in order to improve not only environmental quality but also economic prosperity and social equity for future generations.[10] Next, there is the widely used RESOLVE framework,[11] which describes six actions for the transition to CE: (1) regeneration of ecosystems; (2) sharing of assets; (3) optimising efficiency to reduce waste generation; (4) looping of materials and products; (5) virtualising activities; and (6) exchanging unsustainable materials with more sustainable ones. However, the applicability of this framework to an urban system is limited due to its lack of acknowledgement of the scale, location or context in which these systems operate.[12]

With a growing number of areas of application of the concept, the understanding of CE is increasingly broad,[13] including, for instance, spatial, geopolitical and governance aspects (see chapter 2), social aspects (chapter 3) or environmental regeneration questions

Figure 1.1 The five principles of circular economy (CE)

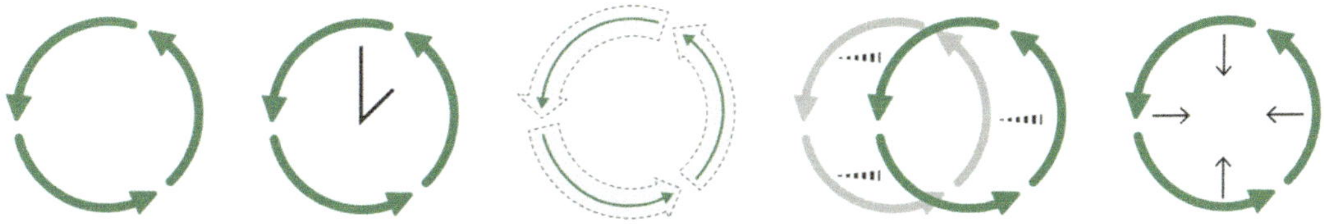

Source: Authors

(chapter 4). But arguably, most definitions of CE emphasise one or more of the following five principles (Figure 1.1):

- A circular flow of materials and energy.
- A slowing down of those flows to keep materials and energy in use for as long as possible at the highest value possible.
- A reduction of the amount of materials and energy used,
- A substitution of non-sustainable materials by sustainable materials that allows for regeneration.
- A geographical concentration of a circular consumption–production system, or localism.[14,15]

1.4 WHY DO CITIES AND REGIONS MATTER?

Cities and regions are particularly relevant for enacting a transition towards CE. Two sectors that consume the most resources are both closely related to cities: construction and mobility.[16] Cities are home to a growing number of people, consuming an increasing amount of goods and generating the bulk of waste. But this also means that urban CE policies can have the greatest impact on global resource consumption and waste production. At a regional scale, there is greater potential to increase resource efficiency if more resources consumed in a region are also produced within that region. Equally, more of the wasted resources could be assimilated within the region. The CE helps with this through the recycling and reuse of existing resources and the generation of renewable energy locally. This could not only help reduce regional global environmental footprints, by cutting down resource consumption and greenhouse gas emissions, but also has the potential to bring new economic opportunities, jobs and revenue to a region, while broadening access to resources that were previously unaffordable to some sections of the population.

Cities and regions also matter for CE because they correspond to relevant scales for the experimentation and implementation of policies and solutions that we need to move away from the current linear economy (take–make–dispose) model in which resources are extracted, used to produce goods and then discarded as waste after use. This reflects the arguments about cities being the critical battleground for dealing with climate change and promoting sustainability transitions, being living laboratories for climate action innovation.[17,18,19,20] Regions and cities are typically more agile and experimental in their policies than the central governments, and this makes them well-equipped to devise innovative policy tools and approaches and coordinate activities between diverse stakeholders to drive sustainability transitions.[21]

Regions and cities are in charge of a broad portfolio of policies that are already in place and need to be coordinated to promote CE, for instance, waste management, economic development, environmental protection, landscape architecture and spatial planning. They also have the capacity to put forward regulations and incentives to adopt more circular practices by industry, using local building codes, spatial plans and planning conditions, contractual agreements, etc. A good example of "tactical" measures to promote CE and stimulate demand for circular construction is local public procurement built around CE principles, which can be a powerful incentive for construction companies to consider changing their practices and adopting circular innovations. Municipal and regional authorities may be involved in the provisioning of infrastructure, energy, food, public transport, waste and water management services, which enables them to adopt CE practices directly. They can also convene networks of stakeholders essential for the delivery of circular systems and build data platforms to inform decision-making. However, subnational governments have varying capacities and resources to enact these actions and stimulate a transition towards CE.[22]

Another factor is that subnational authorities operate "on the ground" and have a better grasp of the local conditions, barriers and enablers of change in regional or local processes.[23] This is an important asset for CE policy, which is affected by contextual features of places such as geographical characteristics, environmental conditions, socio-cultural specificities, economic systems and the presence of industries producing or using specific types of materials. Hard territorial factors such as accessibility and the presence of relevant technologies enable CE operation, while softer territorial factors related to knowledge, the presence of networks and supporting institutions, and awareness of circularity principles and practices among stakeholders are critical for catalysing transitions towards CE.[24,25] All these factors call for designing place-based CE policies to best address the local or regional needs, challenges, and opportunities for looping and restorative actions.

The regional scale is particularly important for such policies. Within regions, a mixture of urban, industrial and rural areas is often present, connected by "hard" infrastructure (for moving people, goods, waste and resources) and "soft" infrastructure (knowledge provision, governance structures and regional innovation ecosystems). The different spatial distribution of economic activity and of the above-mentioned infrastructures in a given region determines the feasible options for stimulating and locating circular activities and enabling symbiotic relationships to develop circular systems.

1.5 CIRCULAR POLICIES IN WANT OF A SPATIAL DIMENSION

The "why" question of the relevance of cities and regions in the CE transition is arguably answered — the next question is "how". There are few templates for urban and regional CE policies. Because of the already mentioned diversity of perspectives on CE, there is also a related diversity of policy discourses on it. While in some policy frameworks CE is considered more holistically, stressing its transformational potential, other policies are based on a narrower and technocentric view, stressing the economic dimension or industrial symbiosis aspects.[26] This diversity reflects the different meanings and values that can be associated with CE and the different approaches to its pursuit, leading to different scenarios according to which CE could be achieved: centralised versus bottom-up approaches; high- versus low-tech solutions; growth versus degrowth models.[27,28] What tends to be overlooked in existing CE policies are spatial questions. There is, however, a growing recognition that the implementation of CE has spatial implications.[29,30] Such a transformation requires fundamental shifts in regional and urban economies, in spatial planning and policymaking, and the behavioural patterns of consumption and dealing with waste.[31,32]

The existing conceptual frameworks that could guide the much-needed shift towards urban and regional development based on CE principles are arguably "footloose", neglecting important (societal) questions on where material flows come from and go to, who drives circular processes and for whom, and what does it take to steer the transition towards positive outcomes in terms of social, economic and environmental sustainability. Consequently, cities and regions implementing CE policies — such as Amsterdam (the Netherlands), Hamburg (Germany), Ghent (Belgium) or Naples (Italy) — face a potent cocktail of political, organisational, spatial, economic and technological barriers for CE transitions. The combinations of those barriers are specific to the different regional or national contexts.[33,34,35,36]

What is more, the declared policy goals related to "going circular" by a given year (e.g., Amsterdam aims to use 50% fewer materials by 2030 and go fully circular by 2050) tend to be quite detached from the reality on the ground and ignore the complexity of transitions towards CE.[37] Instead, many cities and regions are "caught in the circular buzz" — they develop policies that use CE as the new "urban sustainability fix"[38] bringing an illusion that we can shift away from a linear, extractive economy merely by promoting new narratives on waste, new circular business models and closing material loops in selected sectors. The risk is that such actions will remain piecemeal and fail to move cities and regions closer to a CE, which may result in a loss of interest in this concept and the search for the next sustainability "buzzword".

Without a good grasp of what it takes to "go circular" in a given regional or urban territory, of the complexity of this challenge due to the need to collaborate across economic sectors, across scales and levels of government, and overcome major economic, societal and political lock-ins, we risk engaging in "circular washing". In such a case, the CE label may be used to frame strategies and policies that in reality remain limited to the promotion of recycling, build on only the limited use of circular practices or even may favour circularity in some sectors but in a way that is not sustainable (e.g., promoting timber construction in regions that do not produce timber in the Amsterdam region or importing waste from overseas to sustain waste-to-energy schemes in many Nordic cities).

The current "polycrisis"[39] affecting cities and regions as well as the growing socio-economic and territorial disparities that undermine social cohesion and engagement in democratic processes create an urgent need to shed light on the territorial implications of CE and explore ways to tap into transformative potential of this approach. While not a panacea, a spatial perspective on CE does offer the promise of easing some of those pressures. As we argue in this book, integrating a circular perspective into spatial planning and territorial policies can generate a wealth of synergies in the transition to circular futures.

1.6 DEFINING A CIRCULAR CITY AND A CIRCULAR REGION

To consider place-based CE policies for cities and regions, we need to define what a circular city or region actually means. A definition of a circular city is offered by J. Williams.[40] It is a complex, regenerative and adaptive "socio-ecological system, consisting of a bio-geo-physical unit and its associated social actors and institutions" in which three types of circular actions are pursued: (1) looping actions (recycling, reuse, energy recovery, etc.); (2) ecologically regenerative actions (restoring ecosystem and ecosystem services); and (3) adaptive actions that improve the capacity of the urban space and communities to change in the face of new challenges (flexible design and planning, co-creation and learning environment, etc.).

Conceptualisation of a circular region is, however, more challenging. Regions, in general, are notoriously difficult to define. There are different perspectives on what is a region. For example, in defining a region we may consider administrative boundaries, geomorphological systems, perceptions of regional identity and historical legacies. We can also consider patterns of urban agglomeration, industrial networks interconnected by infrastructure, and the much less tangible networks of knowledge and collaboration, interdependencies between the core and periphery where people, companies and economic activities are located, or the rural or peri-urban hinterland where food is produced and resources are extracted. Thus, for the purpose of this book, we define a region as a subnational territorial unit characterised by features such as culture, economy, politics or social structure, delimited by boundaries that

 https://doi.org/10.1080/2578711X.2024.2418227

may be physical (e.g., river basins), administrative (part of a country's territorial system) or functional (based on economic linkages or commuting patterns).

From a CE perspective, the circulation of materials across space and time stands central. Thus, a circular region can be defined through interdependencies and connections created by material flows between the different types of territories (urban, industrial, peri-urban and rural), nature, the built environment and actors. Developing a circular region would, thus, entail adapting the socio-technological and socio-ecological systems so that they could nurture looped systems of materials and energy, helping to regenerate the damaged ecosystems.

From an urban metabolism[41] perspective, a circular region is shaped by the geographies of flows of materials, connecting actors and spaces involved in resource-looping actions that aim at extending the life cycle of products and reduce generation of waste. The boundaries of such circular regions are determined by the interdependent activities related to circular actions, such as recycling, repair or reuse of materials and products, the geographical spread of which can vary depending on the sector of the economy and the material flow. This can be illustrated, for instance, by the geographical spread of construction and demolition waste processing networks in the Amsterdam region (Figure 1.2), concentrated on the periphery of

Figure 1.2 Geography of metabolic material flows in the Amsterdam region of the Netherlands, 2016: networks and clusters of the processing of construction and demolition waste (numbers in circles correspond to activities related to this flow) extend far beyond the administrative boundaries of the region

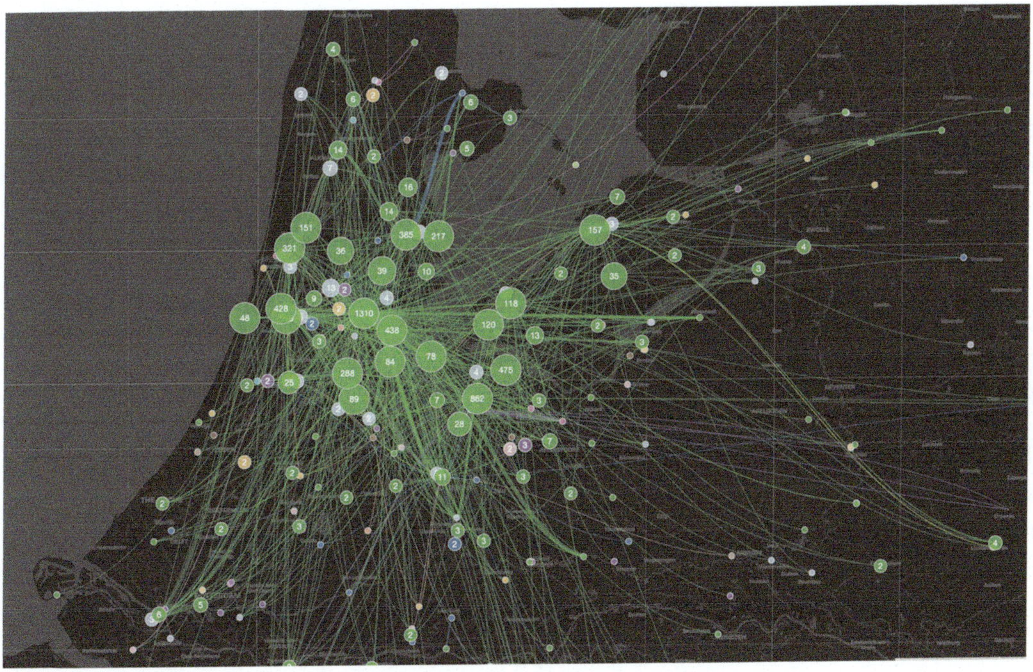

Sources: H2020 REPAiR and H2020 CINDERELA projects

Amsterdam but reaching out to locations spread out across the Province of North Holland and beyond across the Netherlands.

From a regenerative perspective, what matters for circular regions are the natural and constructed green and blue structures. These include rivers and other waterbodies, natural and agricultural landscapes, and urban green areas, which can be regenerated and made more accessible to the inhabitants of the core urban areas and of their hinterland through circular activities to restore ecosystems and provide ecosystem services.

Finally, from an adaptive perspective, a circular region is a relational space in which the diverse stakeholders — ranging from spatial planners, regional policy actors, research and education institutions, companies, non-governmental organisations, and citizens — can collaborate, co-produce strategies, plans and policies, and engage in learning and exchange of knowledge across administrative, disciplinary and sectoral boundaries, which are needed to develop circular solutions tailored to the regional context. From this perspective, what matters are not only the material flows but also the flows of knowledge and information through networks of CE actors.

1.7 KNOWLEDGE AND POLICY GAPS

Such a circular perspective on urban and regional spaces has several policy implications. When planning and designing policies to promote a transition towards circular cities and regions, we need to go beyond the narrow focus on the city and its metabolism and, instead, reconsider the relations between the (urban) core and the peri-urban space (where industrial actors and waste management activities tend to concentrate) and the rural periphery (where especially organic materials originate from and where the by-products of consumption of those materials in the city can be revalorised). In other words, a circular perspective on a city or region invites us to rebalance the relationship between the core and periphery, which is currently skewed towards the cities, placing an emphasis on the crucial role of the hinterland from a metabolic perspective. This, in turn, requires rethinking regional planning and governance to consider circular interdependencies and complementarities across the regional space, as well as embracing "soft planning" approaches for functional circular regions. However, we still lack insight into and successful examples of how to achieve this in practice.

There is an emerging scholarly literature on circular transitions in cities and regions,[42] on spatial planning for circularity,[43,44,45] on frameworks for circular urban development,[46,47] on the role of the regional scale,[48,49] on bottom-up action in these processes[50,51] and on participatory experimentation to promote development of a circular built environment.[52] Most of the research on CE, however, remains concerned with the waste management sector and the most basic circular actions focusing on energy recovery from waste (e.g., waste incineration to produce electric energy and heat) and recycling (i.e., transforming waste into raw materials that can be used to manufacture new products), overlooking the more demanding strategies towards extension of the life cycle of products and eventually reduction of waste generated that could have more far-reaching impacts on the transitions towards a more sustainable society.[53] The same holds true for policy practice. Innovative circular practices and interventions have been rapidly spreading in cities across Europe and globally, including those that aim at the transformation of the built environment and the promotion of environmental and social sustainability, even if they tend to remain rather niche and are hardly promoted in spatial planning and urban policies. In fact, CE strategies and policies do proliferate rapidly, but tend to focus on waste management[54] or a piecemeal "circular fix",[55] seldom taking spatial, regenerative, governance and social aspects into account.[56] There is very little thinking about what kind of CE we actually want to pursue, how, where and, importantly, for whom.

There is a gap between scientific insights on the transformative potential of CE and policy on the ground. Policymakers tend to reduce CE to a "zero waste" approach, based on recycling or industrial symbiosis, and expect it to help achieve sustainability goals, while generating economic growth, innovation and jobs. Moreover, there are disparities in terms of knowledge and capacity to design place-based CE policies across countries and regions. We can already see huge gaps in progress towards CE across the European Union, for instance,[57] with highly industrialised countries of Western and Northern Europe leading the way. Even when we zoom into the regions that are leading in terms of engagement with circular business models and employment in CE,[58,59] we notice that there are substantial differences in the degree of engagement with the CE concept in policy across municipalities and among businesses.[60]

The transition towards CE may, thus, deepen intra- and interregional disparities, with the already more developed and resourceful territories being able to jump onto the CE bandwagon and the lagging ones finding themselves falling even more behind. It also brings forward the question of how to transfer knowledge on place-based CE policies effectively and develop the capacity of all regions and cities to engage in transition towards more circular future. Finally, if we are to avoid "circular washing" and measure and monitor the state of play in CE transitions and the impacts of circular policy innovations, we need to develop new metrics and benchmarking tools. These need to reflect the complexity of CE transitions in urban and regional contexts and be based on relevant data not only on material flows across space but also on the impacts of circular innovations in terms of spatial change, institutional capacities, social cohesion, and even awareness and behavioural shifts among companies and citizens.

1.8 CONCLUSIONS

CE is a promising approach that could nudge cities and regions towards more sustainable development. In this chapter, we highlighted the importance of cities and regions in the transition towards CE and made a case for considering an often-overlooked spatial perspective on these shifts. Adopting such a spatial lens is needed to understand better the territorial impacts of "going circular", create the spatial conditions for circular activities, and harness the transformative and regenerative potential of this approach by moving beyond zero-waste strategies and implementing holistic, context-specific CE policies that combine economic, social and environmental dimensions of sustainability. Having defined a circular city and a circular region through the lens of resource flows and the regenerative and adaptive potentials of territorialised circular strategies, we outlined the remaining knowledge gaps and proposed a policy and research agenda to bridge them. The building blocks of this agenda are discussed in the remainder of this book.

Practitioner's perspective

Our experience of working with local and regional authorities shows that they do start to embrace the circular economy (CE) concept, but it is sometimes perceived as utopian. A peculiarity of local government action is the focus on implementation "within the administrative boundaries", which makes it challenging for them to work on the reduction of waste within value chains that go beyond those boundaries.

An additional difficulty is the need to incorporate multiple actors into circular processes. Formal constraints on such cross-sectoral and cross-boundary collaborations, the relative novelty of the CE approach, and uncertainties about pilot activities (which are not always successful) raise concerns and hinder adopting holistic approaches to process planning for regional and local circular strategies and projects.

Subnational governments are not always willing to experiment, however; they are keener to innovate with CE by pursuing "smaller steps". It is also important for them that the benefits of actions to promote CE can be perceived in the short term, ideally with their success announced during the term of office of the local or regional authority.

A Living Lab methodology, increasingly used across many cities and regions to co-design innovative place-based solutions, allows for the gradual expose of diverse local actors to principles of CE and engaging them in joint experiments with circular development in a real-world setting. The challenge, though, is how to build on such participatory experimentation and "anchor" this approach in local and regional policies and planning. The CE approach may "take hold" if it is explicitly formulated — in a development strategy or other planning document — as a goal and a means to achieve sustainability, a concept that subnational authorities already know and understand.

Maciej Kowalczyk and Małgorzata Grodzicka-Kowalczyk *are founders of PHENO HORIZON, a consulting company focusing on regional and local development in Łódź, Poland*

 https://doi.org/10.1080/2578711X.2024.2418227

NOTES

1 IUCN (2023) *Cities and Nature*. Issue brief. Gland, Switzerland: International Union for Conservation of Nature and Natural Resources. https://iucn.org/resources/issues-brief/cities-and-nature

2 Dobbs R, Manyika J, Woetzel L, Remes J, Perrey J, Kelly G, Pattabiraman K and Sharma H (2016) *Urban World: The Global Consumers to Watch*. McKinsey Global Institute. https://www.mckinsey.com/featured-insights/urbanization/urban-world-the-global-consumers-to-watch

3 Williams J (2021) *Circular Cities: A Revolution in Urban Sustainability*. Abingdon: Routledge. https://doi.org/10.4324/9780429490613

4 Williams J (2019) Circular cities. *Urban Studies*, 56(13): 2746–2762. https://doi.org/10.1177/0042098018806133

5 Kirchherr J (2023) Bullshit in the sustainability and transitions literature: A provocation. *Circular Economy and Sustainability*, 3: 167–172. https://doi.org/10.1007/s43615-022-00175-9.

6 Kirchherr J, Reike D and Hekkert M (2017) Conceptualizing the circular economy: An analysis of 114 definitions. *Resources, Conservation and Recycling*, 127: 221–232. https://doi.org/10.1016/j.resconrec.2017.09.005

7 Ellen MacArthur Foundation (EMF) and McKinsey & Co. (2012) *Towards the Circular Economy*, Vol. 1: *An Economic and Business Rationale for an Accelerated Transition*. EMF and McKinsey & Co. https://www.ellenmacarthurfoundation.org/towards-the-circular-economy-vol-1-an-economic-and-business-rationale-for-an

8 Williams (2021), see Reference 3.

9 Williams (2019), see Reference 4.

10 Kirchherr et al. (2017), see Reference 6.

11 EMF and McKinsey & Co. (2012), see Reference 7.

12 Williams (2021), Reference 3.

13 Cf. Corvellec H, Stowell A F and Johansson N (2022. Critiques of the circular economy. *Journal of Industrial Ecology, 26*(2): 421–432. https://doi.org/10.1111/jiec.13187

14 North P (2010) Eco-localisation as a progressive response to peak oil and climate change — A sympathetic critique. *Geoforum*, 41(4): 585–594. https://doi.org/10.1016/j.geoforum.2009.04.013

15 Van den Berghe K and Verhagen T (2021) Making it concrete: Analysing the role of concrete plants' locations for circular city policy goals. *Frontiers in Built Environment*, 7, Article 748842. https://doi.org/10.3389/fbuil.2021.748842

16 Circle Economy (2023) *The Circularity Gap Report 2023*. Amsterdam: Circle Economy.

17 Castán Broto V and Bulkeley H (2013) A survey of urban climate change experiments in 100 cities. *Global Environmental Change*, 23(1): 92–102. https://doi.org/10.1016/j.gloenvcha.2012.07.005

18 Castán Broto V and Westman L K (2020) Ten years after Copenhagen: Reimagining climate change governance in urban areas. *WIREs Climate Change, 11*(4), e643. https://doi.org/10.1002/wcc.643

19 von Wirth T, Frantzeskaki N and Loorbach D (2020) Urban living labs as inter-boundary spaces for sustainability transitions? In G de Roo, C Yamu and C Zuidema (eds.), *Handbook on Planning and Complexity*, pp. 237–257. Cheltenham, UK: Edward Elgar. https://doi.org/10.4337/9781786439185.00017

20 Frantzeskaki N, Broto V C, Coenen L and Loorbach D (2017) *Urban Sustainability Transitions: The Dynamics and Opportunities of Sustainability Transitions in Cities, in Urban Sustainability Transitions*, pp. 1–20. Abingdon: Routledge.

21 Arsova S, Genovese A and Ketikidis P H (2022) Implementing circular economy in a regional context: A systematic literature review and a research agenda. *Journal of Cleaner Production*, 368: 133117. https://doi.org/10.1016/j.jclepro.2022.133117

22 Williams (2021), Reference 3.

23 Arsova et al. (2022), see Reference 21.

24 Tapia C, Bianchi M, Pallaske G and Bassi A M (2021) Towards a territorial definition of a circular economy: Exploring the role of territorial factors in closed-loop systems. *European Planning Studies*: 29(8): 1438–1457. https://doi.org/10.1080/09654313.2020.1867511

25 ESPON (2019) *CIRCTER — Circular Economy and Territorial Consequences*. https://archive.espon.eu/circular-economy

26 For an overview, see Calisto Friant M, Vermeulen W J and Salomone R (2020) A typology of circular economy discourses: Navigating the diverse visions of a contested paradigm. *Resources, Conservation and Recycling*, 161: 104917. https://doi.org/10.1016/j.resconrec.2020.104917

27 Williams (2021), Reference 3.

28 Bauwens T, Hekkert M and Kirchherr J (2020) Circular futures: What will they look like? *Ecological Economics*, 175: 106703. https://doi.org/j.ecolecon.2020.106703

29 van Bueren E, Buizer M, Van den Berghe K B J, Heijkers B, Meijs L, Verhagen T, Dittrich K and Sprecher B (2022) *Perspectieven op circulaire gebiedsontwikkeling: Lessen uit de Binckhorst en andere gebiedsontwikkelingen*. The Hague: Accelerating the Circular Economy Zuid-Holland (ACCEZ). https://pure.tudelft.nl/ws/portalfiles/portal/115361379/Eindrapportage_Circulaire_gebiedsontwikkeling.pdf

30 Van den Berghe K and Vos M (2019) Circular area design or circular area functioning? A discourse-institutional analysis of circular area developments in Amsterdam and Utrecht, The Netherlands. *Sustainability*, 11(18): 4875. https://doi.org/10.3390/su11184875

31 Williams (2021), Reference 3.

32 Williams J (2023) Circular cities: Planning for circular development in European cities. *European Planning Studies*, 31(1): 14–35. https://doi.org/10.1080/09654313.2022.2060707

33 Obersteg A, Arlati A, Acke A, Berruti G, Czapiewski K, Dąbrowski M, Heurkens E, Mezei C, Palestino M F, Varju V, Wójcik M and Knieling J (2019) Urban regions shifting to circular economy: Understanding challenges for new ways of governance. *Urban Planning*, 4(3): 19–31. https://doi.org/10.17645/up.v4i3.2158

34 Heurkens E and Dąbrowski M (2020) Circling the square: Governance of the circular economy transition in the Amsterdam Metropolitan Area. *European Spatial Research and Policy*, 27(2): 11–31. https://doi.org/10.18778/1231-1952.27.2.02

35 Russell M, Gianoli A and Grafakos S (2020) Getting the ball rolling: An exploration of the drivers and barriers towards the implementation of bottom-up circular economy initiatives in Amsterdam and Rotterdam. *Journal of Environmental Planning and Management*: 63(11): 1903–1926. https://doi.org/10.1080/09640568.2019.1690435

36 Dagilienė L, Varaniūtė V and Bruneckienė J (2021) Local governments' perspective on implementing the circular economy: A framework for future solutions. *Journal of Cleaner Production*, 310: 127340. https://doi.org/10.1016/j.jclepro.2021.127340

37 Calisto Friant M, Vermeulen W J V and Salomone R (2021) Analysing European Union circular economy policies: Words versus actions. *Sustainable Production and Consumption*, 27: 337–353. https://doi.org/10.1016/j.spc.2020.11.001

38 Kębłowski W, Lambert D and Bassens D (2020) Circular economy and the city: An urban political economy agenda. *Culture and Organization*, 26(2): 142–158. https://doi.org/10.1080/14759551.2020.1718148

39 Tooze A (2022, 28 October) Welcome to the world of the polycrisis. *Financial Times*. https://www.ft.com/content/498398e7-11b1-494b-9cd3-6d669dc3de33

40 Williams (2021), see Reference 3.

41 Urban metabolism is a concept used for exploring the flow of materials and energy within a city or an urban region, building on the metaphor of an urban area as a living organism. It considers resource input (water, energy, raw materials, etc.), their transformation through urban activities (e.g., construction, transportation, consumption), and the output of waste and emissions. In this book, we understand urban metabolism through a regional lens, acknowledging that the flows related to activities within a city extend beyond the boundaries of the urban area to peri-urban and rural areas, as well as to other regions (Figure 2).

42 Prendeville S, Cherim E and Bocken N (2018) Circular cities: Mapping six cities in transition. *Environmental Innovation and Societal Transitions*, 26: 171–194. https://doi.org/10.1016/j.eist.2017.03.002

43 Williams (2023), see Reference 32.

44 Remøy H, Wandl A, Ceric D and van Timmeren A (2019) Facilitating circular economy in urban planning. *Urban Planning*, 4(3): 1–4. https://doi.org/10.17645/up.v4i3.2484

45 Turcu C and Gillie H (2020) Governing the circular economy in the city: Local planning practice in London. *Planning Practice & Research*, 35(1): 62–85. https://doi.org/10.1080/02697459.2019.1703335

46 van Bueren et al. (2022), see Reference 29.

47 Williams J (2020) The role of spatial planning in transitioning to circular urban development. *Urban Geography*, 41(6): 915–919. https://doi.org/10.1080/02723638.2020.1796042

48 Arsova et al. (2022), see Reference 21.

49 Van den Berghe K, Bucci Ancapi F and van Bueren E (2020) When a fire starts to burn. The relation between an (inter)nationally oriented incinerator capacity and the port cities' local circular ambitions. *Sustainability*, 12(12): 4889. https://www.mdpi.com/2071-1050/12/12/4889

50 Russell et al. (2019), see Reference 35.

51 Termeer C J A M and Metze T A P (2019) More than peanuts: Transformation towards a circular economy through a small-wins governance framework. *Journal of Cleaner Production*, 240: 118272. https://doi.org/10.1016/j.jclepro.2019.118272

52 Amenta L, Attademo A, Remøy H, Berruti G, Cerreta M, Formato E, Palestino M F and Russo M (2019) Managing the transition towards circular metabolism: Living labs as a co-creation approach. *Urban Planning*, 4(3): 5–18. https://doi.org/10.17645/up.v4i3.2170

53 Vanhuyse F, Fejzić E, Ddiba D and Henrysson M (2021) The lack of social impact considerations in transitioning towards urban circular economies: a scoping review. *Sustainable Cities and Society*, 75, 103394. https://doi.org/10.1016/j.scs.2021.103394

54 Dagilienė et al. (2021), see Reference 36.

55 Kębłowski et al. (2020),see Reference 38.

56 Williams (2020), see Reference 47.

57 Mazur-Wierzbicka E (2021) Towards circular economy — A comparative analysis of the countries of the European Union. *Resources*, 10(5): 49. https://doi.org/10.3390/resources10050049

58 ESPON (2019), see Reference 25.

59 ESPON (2022) *Policy brief: A territorial approach to transitioning towards a circular economy.* https://archive.espon.eu/topics-policy/publications/policy-brief-territorial-approach-transitioning-towards-circular-economy

60 Heurkens and Dąbrowski (2020), see Reference 34.

2. The window of opportunity for circular economy in Europe in the wake of the geopolitical turmoil: connecting scales and principles

Karel Van den Berghe and Marcin Dąbrowski

Keywords: circular economy; geopolitics; spatial planning; localism; European Union

Wind turbines in the fields. *Source*: Thomas Richter, https://unsplash.com/photos/aerial-photo-of-wind-turbines-near-field-B09tL5bSQJk

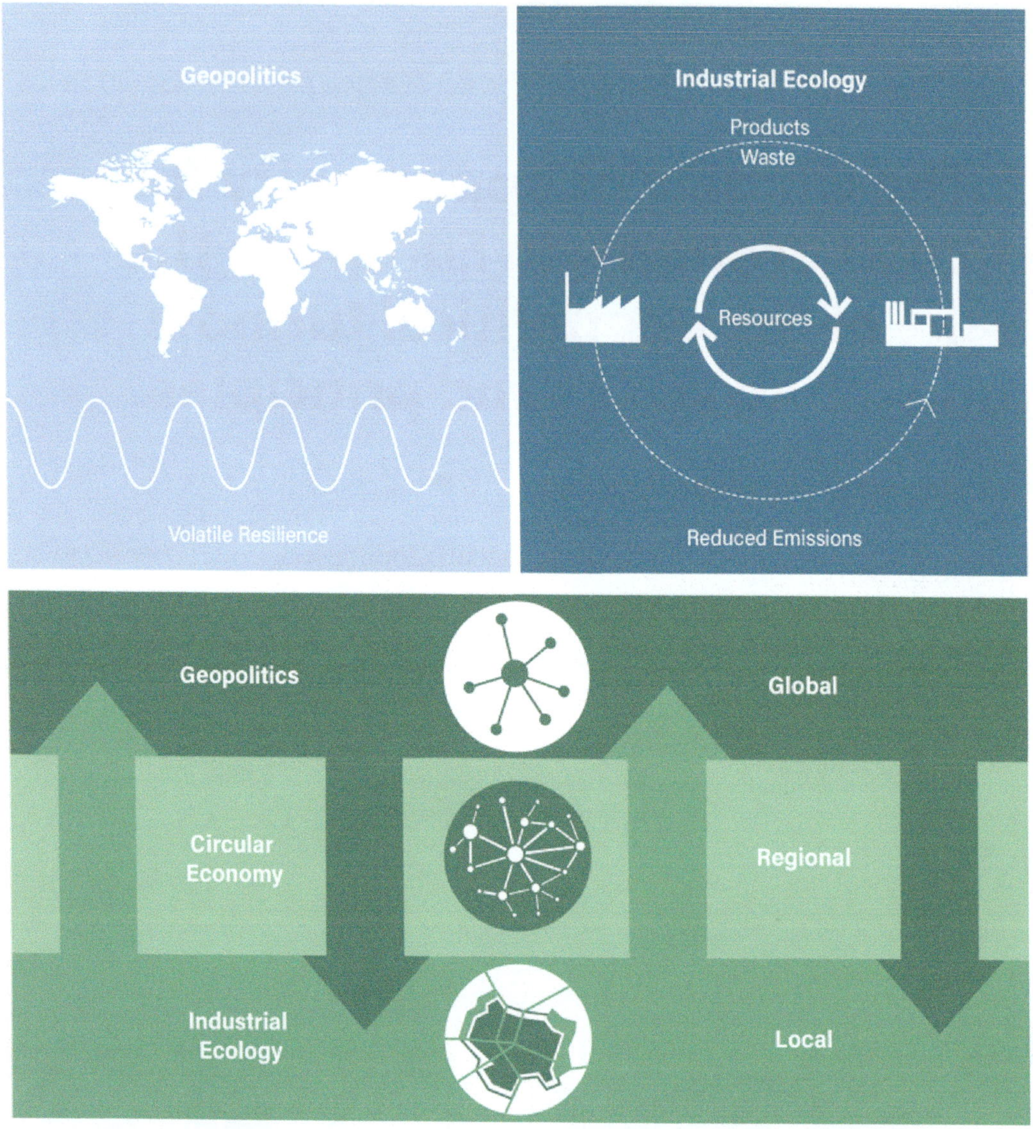

Source: Authors; graphic design by Fábio Alzate Martinez (TU Delft)

https://doi.org/10.1080/2578711X.2024.2418228

Key message

The current geopolitical turmoil offers a unique opportunity to leverage the circular economy as a strategy to reduce dependencies and enhance economic, social, and ecological resilience by localising production and reusing revaluing materials.

2.1 OVERVIEW

One of the five circular economy (CE) principles is "localisation" or "localism", understood as a smaller geographical consumption–production system that fits better with local needs. Rightfully, the rationale for localism is derived from ecological principles. However, these arguments remain debated and subsequently can fail to become operationalised in policy goals and measures. From a governance perspective, localism is perhaps the most important CE principle, as it is the only one that clearly links the circulation of resources to a confined area, and so to specific administrative areas, and eventually informs us "who is responsible", and so will have the advantages, but also the disadvantages, of CE. In this chapter, we turn our attention to the European context, where the European Union (EU) and many of its member states have set out an ambitious policy agenda for moving towards CE. We argue that the current geopolitical turmoil provides a "window of opportunity" through which to clarify the responsibilities for driving a transition towards CE across levels of government and to seize the momentum to operationalise the localism principle and move European cities and regions towards more resilient, circular futures.

2.2 WE ARE AT WAR(S)!

> Can Europe form a nation by deciding to depend on the material conditions that it pretended to ignore during the period of false peace in which it believed itself to be? (Bruno Latour)[1]

In his last paper, entitled "Is Europe's soil changing beneath our feet?" (2022), the French social scientist Bruno Latour argues that two "wars" are currently coming together: the war on climate change and the geopolitical war. He continues that both are, in essence, territorial wars, although the war on climate change was hardly perceived as such. The war on climate has been characterised by "non-action", which is in stark contrast to the territorial war ongoing in Ukraine which — for many, unexpectedly — brought about rapid geopolitical shifts and a strong response from the West (e.g., sanctions, weapons supply). But at least in one aspect, the two wars have become connected, and that is via Russian gas and oil. Suddenly, these strategic Russian resources became something that the European states should avoid paying for, as it directly funds the Russian aggression. But at the same

https://doi.org/10.1080/2578711X.2024.2418228

time, this crisis put forward the need to accelerate the switch to more sustainable energy sources. Hence, the two territorial conflicts converge. And this brings "an incredible [window of] opportunity to be seized, which is redefining the territorial situation in the dual form of border defence and energy autonomy".[2]

In this chapter, echoing the arguments raised by Latour, we focus on the implications of the shift towards CE for the EU. The EU has been at the forefront of emerging policies to promote resource efficiency and CE as a means of moving towards more sustainable futures. For instance, the EU has put forward its Circular Economy Action Plan as one of the building blocks of the wider sustainability transition agenda promoted by the European Green Deal.[3,4] This perspective is also reflected in the national policies of several EU member states. However, as we argued in chapter 1, both European and national policies tend to overlook the spatial implications of CE. Therefore, we reflect on this window of opportunity in which sustainability policy goals — particularly the transitions towards a CE — can finally be implemented by emphasising the role of space and territorial development in these transitions[5,6] within the European context. Indeed, policies that aim to cope with climate change and other ecological disasters — in some cases broadened to include economic and social goals, too — have been implemented within the European bloc at least since the "Club of Rome"[7] 50 years ago. However, we can safely argue that these policy goals have not been accomplished so far. Quite the contrary is true.

Taking the above into account, this chapter focuses on the last of the five CE principles outlined in chapter 1: localisation or localism, but not local per se.[8] The localism principles assume that economic (spatial) decisions should meet the needs as locally as possible.[9] "Local" here is not seen as an ideological starting point (whereby autarkic systems would be promoted to ensure that localities become self-sufficient by producing and managing their own resources without relying on flows from other localities), but as an end result, especially when taking into account the labour and environmental standards left out in many economic decisions .[10] In other words, a CE with the localism principle in mind strives for a production–consumption system that is as local as possible. Such reasoning thus implies the need to include space into the discussion of CE. However, the CE principle of localism is far from easy to realise in policy practice. Indeed, including labour and especially environmental and climate change considerations into spatial economic decisions is not a standard governance practice, and leads to a more normative or, perhaps, more realistic perspective on a circular city or region.

Conceptually, the difficulty in addressing climate change is that it is a global phenomenon (e.g., CO_2 increase) with (very) local and often temporary, although increasingly structural, effects, whereas governmental organisations, which are in general in the lead to drive climate policies, are territorially confined.[11] This makes policymaking vulnerable to "externalisation" of the problem by shifting it to a different location outside of one's jurisdiction or to its periphery. In turn this can lead to "green-washing" or "cherry-picking" the benefits and not the burdens, whereby governments at national and subnational levels dodge the actions that are effectively necessary to cope with the (global) ecological challenges, despite ambitious discourse on climate change mitigation. For example, Copenhagen in Denmark is regarded as one of the leading cities on planning for sustainability. However, as shown by Krähmer,[12] Copenhagen's strategy for climate neutrality is based on the externalisation of that problem. Specifically, Copenhagen's policy only accounts for the greenhouse gas emissions emitted in Copenhagen itself. In that light, moving polluting activities out of Copenhagen is a logical course of action to reach policy targets. Obviously, this does not imply that these activities "magically" disappear. They are merely displaced beyond the city's administrative boundaries.[13]

Therefore, building on the opening quotation from Latour,[14] in what follows we will explain the window of opportunity between the "place-oriented" geopolitics based on a "us versus them" logic and the currently footloose sustainability policy implementation that could be spatially grounded via the concept of CE, the latest sustainability idea that has been gaining traction. We argue that space, and thus the localism principle, has much promise if it stands central in the CE policy discourse as it can help solve the decades-long standstill in sustainability progress. If policymakers do not take advantage of this window of opportunity wherein the two territorial conflicts converge and create scope for driving place-based circular policies, the whole CE agenda risks losing momentum. This, in turn, would undermine all the efforts of public and private organisations to promote circularity so far, and foremost all the potential it brings to improve social equity and biodiversity, which is identified on top of the "core" discourse on looping material flows. Conversely, the efforts to address the geopolitical challenge of redefining "Europe" as an entity that is less vulnerable to re-/de-globalisation and the growing geopolitical tensions could benefit from incorporating CE principles.

2.3 FORTRESS CIRCULAR ECONOMY: FROM A NEGATIVE TO A POSITIVE NARRATIVE?

Obviously, the geography of flows of tangible and intangible resources can be understood in many ways, conceptually ranging from a complete global perspective on flows of resources[15] to a local autarkic system.[16,17] We do not have space here to elaborate much on this, but we want to point out the existence of networked cross-boundary or cross-sectoral spatial systems and their geography, which are always normative and conditioned by the relations between local and global actors, assets and institutions.[18] Those divergent interpretations of CE and perspectives on the geography of flows of resources have been examined within the CE literature.[19] Four CE discourses are defined: (1) a reformist circular society that strives for economic prosperity within the planetary boundaries (cf. doughnut economics proposed by Raworth[20]); (2) a transformational circular society that completely reconfigures the current socio-political system to drastically reduce humanity's ecological footprint, though in harmony with everyone and with the Earth; (3) a techno-centric CE that strives for green growth based on ecological modernisation; and (4) a fortress CE that considers the reform of capitalism impossible and mistrusts socio-technical innovations, but instead tries to maintain geostrategic resource security within a given relational space.

Calisto Friant et al.[21] label the "fortress circular economy" as quite a negative, cynical discourse that is not engaging with the mainstream debate. Also in the literature on the CE, only 4% of the scholarly articles relate to this discourse, while the majority debate transformational circular society (42%), reformist circular society (28%) or technocentric CE (26%).[22] This is in stark contrast to the perspective of Latour.[23] Even though he does not literally use the same "fortress" discourse, he sees this idea as an opportunity that finally can lead to a European nation built on ecological principles. Or, in other words, if we follow Latour's argument, exactly the ignoring or even negative labelling of a geographically confined understanding of a CE is a main reason why a CE, or sustainability in general, is not achieved. Thus, a "fortress CE" idea perhaps has potential if seen from a positive instead of a negative perspective.

2.4 SCALES OF CIRCULAR ECONOMY APPLICATIONS

There are some challenges with such a perspective, though. The discourse "fortress CE" can quickly become a synonym for an autarkic system. Understood as such, the local, as opposed to the global, or footloose understanding of a CE can indeed be problematic in many ways and have even a negative ecological impact. The misunderstanding is that a "localised" or "fortress CE" should not be understood in its narrow (Newtonian) perspective, but rather from a relational perspective. As such, a "fortress CE" is a CE that embraces "localism" as a means, not as a goal (cf. local). Localism, as defined by North[24] or Curtis,[25] was originally reasoned upon labour and environmental standards, but increasingly also resource security, research and development (R&D), and even norms and values are making the outcome of localism more prominent. The challenge here is, as Latour[26] argues, not to tip the balance completely the other way so that geopolitical resource scarcity becomes the main driver of localism, and thus becomes basically a strict understanding of the local, while ecological standards are in some cases left out of the policy. To understand this arguably rapid change related to localism in reference to CE, we briefly overview the different CE applications. In this, we focus on the scale at which the application of CE has an impact or for which CE policies are designed. We understand scales here not merely from a geographical perspective, but also from an institutional perspective (thus also as tiers or levels of government).

The relatively short history of CE applications has started at both "extremes" of the geographical scales, namely the local and the global (Figure 2.1). First, the local scale refers to the scale of a building or its components or specific consumer products. The first "circular" products — rolled out in the 2010s — designed with CE principles and successfully commercialised

Figure 2.1 Different scales of CE applications, their start at both the local and the global, how they gradually are up- or downscaling, and their convergence at the urban and regional scales

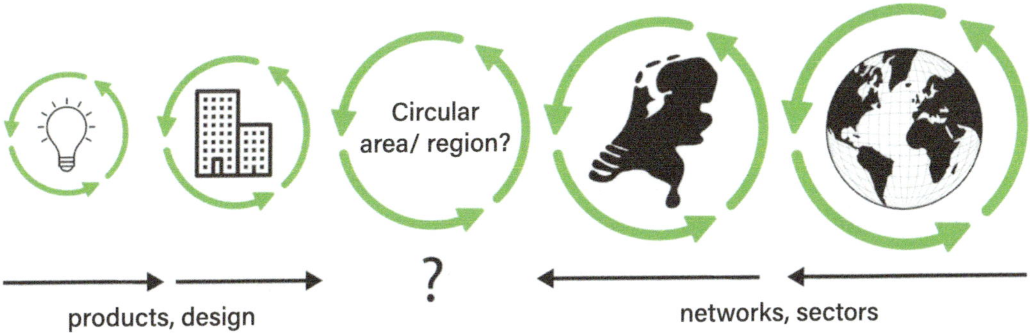

Source: van Bueren et al. (2022)[27]

included, for example, lighting as a service (cf. Philips), modular smart phones, clothes made from plastic waste, or bio-based, modular or recycled building materials. Soon these circular principles were being upscaled, and today circular cars and entire circularly designed and constructed buildings and infrastructures emerge. Gradually, CE principles have an impact on an ever-larger scale, as by now we observe first applications at the neighbourhood scale and ambitions by cities to "go circular" within three decades (cf. Amsterdam's policy).[28] Most likely, this trend will continue, and gradually circular design principles will impact even larger scales — that of a region or even a country.[29] Examples are strategies for development of circular urban food systems, or circular tendering policies by cities. At this point, the CE applications thus increasingly become less technical and more related to societal and political systemic questions.

Second, CE principles were initially applied at a global scale. Here the CE application is an arguably abstract policy goal. First appointed as an important strategy in China at the beginning of this century,[30] more than 10 years later the European Commission also emphasised its importance in its 2015 Circular Economy Action plan,[31] soon followed by the Organisation for Economic Co-operation and Development (OECD),[32] etc. But also private globally orientated organisations, such as the Ellen MacArthur Foundation,[33] successfully popularised the concept around the world. Arguably, the emphasis of these global CE policies was dominantly related to sustainability, seeing the CE as a strategy to help achieve the long-set sustainable policy goals. This CE policy emphasising sustainability has then travelled "downwards" through the scales. Indeed, increasingly, in recent years, national governments, such as of EU member states, started to mention CE in their national policy documents. In parallel, regions and cities joined the cause with a proliferation of urban and regional CE policies and actions to promote CE principles. Arguably, while more developed and affluent cities were front-runners of this trend (Amsterdam, Paris, London, Ghent, Toronto, etc.), the concept of CE is embraced by a growing number of local governments in large and smaller cities around the world. At present, many cities engage in the redevelopment of urban neighbourhoods using CE principles.[34] Therefore, the abstract CE policy goals become increasingly territorialised,[35] and efforts are undertaken to integrate them into day-to-day spatial planning activities.

In sum, the CE applications that started, on the one hand, as a local technical exercise and as an abstract global policy goal, on the other, are coming together at the regional, urban or neighbourhood scales. It is no longer a technical or a policy challenge, but it is both. And therefore, it becomes a spatial challenge. Conceptually, this confluence can be understood as a spatial network or systemic/societal challenge, wherein the built environment, materials and products become connected to relational policy, sectoral, governance issues.

2.5 LOCALISM AS A RESULT OF THE GEOPOLITICAL TURMOIL

The convergence of scales, the convergence of technology and abstract policymaking, and the conceptual convergence between space and networks is increasingly challenged by a geopolitical "reality check" following the recent turmoil for Europe to which Latour[36] refers. Arguably, before the geopolitical crisis started, the effective spatial planning of the convergence between scales was mostly dominated by an arguably "nice-to-have" or even "greenwashing" CE area development. The latter is understood as an area development based on CE ideas, but foremost focusing on dense urban areas, while still externalising the land-use functions, such as waste treatment, to the periphery.[37,38] The Copenhagen example introduced above is illustrative of this.[39] Nonetheless, achieving CE principles is not a "free lunch". Especially in Europe, it is increasingly realised that (re)manufacturing, waste treatment, logistics, (sustainable) energy and (biobased) materials have a certain spatial demand and take place at a certain location, which can, in some cases, come with local burdens, such as greenhouse gas emissions, noise or odours. Externalising these was for decades the easiest way for many cities, or even for the entire EU. But if borders close and disruptions in global flows of resources and products occur due to geopolitical pressures, then suddenly achieving the desired outcomes of CE policies, such as the circular design of cars or residential areas, is no longer possible. Hence, we have come to a moment of reckoning.

Gradually, we can see signs of that reckoning in policy reports and documents. Increasingly, the dominant "just-in-time" organisational principle, the hallmark of global production networks,[40] is being replaced by the "just-in-case" principle.[41,42] Suddenly, the spatial costs derived from the far-from-efficient use of space following an inventory with (long-time) stored materials and products (e.g., face masks), or a vast reserve of (national) energy (cf. gas market disruptions), are no longer questioned. While the current discussions are mostly related to energy and specific supply chains, increasingly such geopolitical reasoning will be linked to CE,[43] forcing us to realise and plan how regions and spatial functions relate to each other, who gets the benefits and bears the burdens of a transition towards a CE.[44,45,46]

In this perspective, it is illustrative that, for example, in the EU's recent report on the performance of science, research and innovation, it is stated that more circularity, and specifically the establishment or reshoring of the production of, for example, clean energy equipment, is needed to reduce the EU's strategic dependencies. Though the report also states that "the EU should avoid sacrificing international welfare gains".[47] In this example, we see exactly the desired confluence between geopolitics and socio-economic and ecological principles that Latour[48] appoints as the window of opportunity between the two wars. The question, though, remains if and how fast this "new" labelling of the CE on the global end of the CE applications will travel down to the urban and regional levels. Even though, as we pointed out, at this level the CE territorialisation is increasingly challenged by the geopolitical "reality check", there is a risk that this realisation is not fast enough to fully take advantage of this window of opportunity.

2.6 THE LOCALISM PRINCIPLE OF CIRCULAR ECONOMY IS THE MOST IMPORTANT ONE

The central argument of this chapter is that there is an opportunity to exploit in the conjunction of two wars with which Europe is confronted: the war against climate change (ecological war) and the war against Europe and the West waged by Vladimir Putin's Russia (military and economic war). We explained that the CE concept is (increasingly) a potential strategy in both these wars, respectively, to achieve the reduction of ecological impact and the decrease of geopolitical dependency by reusing materials, but in (spatial) practice these goals are conflicting. Arguably, the war against climate change that we have been fighting for decades is failing because the cause and the problem are not (always) at the same location, resulting in institutional ambiguity about who should take responsibility for concrete actions against climate change, manifested even on a local urban scale (cf. the Copenhagen example). The result is the externalisation of the burdens of urban sustainability measures (e.g., waste treatment), which remains commonplace.

Currently, the growing interest in the CE concept at the urban and regional scales, leading to its effective territorialisation or integration into spatial planning practice, leads to a continuation of this externalisation trend. What is often chosen are "nice-to-have" CE spatial planning actions, such as the circular design of residential buildings or neighbourhoods, the promotion of small-scale repair cafés, etc., instead of in many cases tackling the core urban CE activities, such as waste treatment, logistics or remanufacturing.[49,50,51] This spatial policymaking in many cities and regions is, to some extent, logical and a result of how decades of globalisation have structured spatial global production networks.[52] But with the geopolitical "shock" that we described, European policymakers realise that open borders and externalisation of the burdens of sustainability are no longer an option. The continuing war in Ukraine, arguably a proxy war against Europe and the West, is showing how dependent Europe is on the external supply of energy, on the provision of defence, and the import of products and resources. In this perspective, the CE concept can be seen as a strategy to reduce these critical dependencies. Or, in other words, if Europe can reuse the material stocks and products it already has or manufactures, it no longer needs to import those from more or less hostile countries around the world. However, at present, this potential role of CE remains overlooked in policy debates.

Figure 2.2 Convergence of the upscaling of the circularity–technological local perspective and the downscaling of the abstract global CE policies' scales on the principle of localism. If successful, localism can become the much-needed acceleration of the other four CE principles, in the end helping to achieve long-desired social and ecological goals

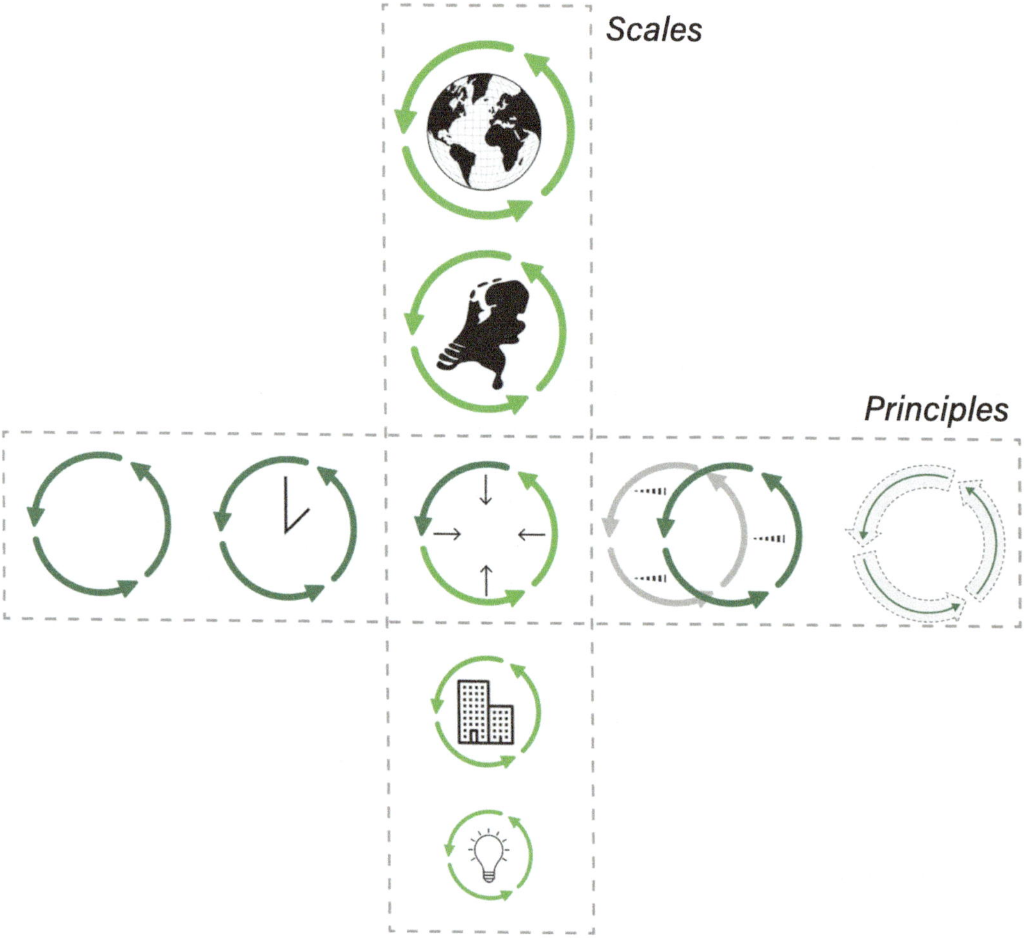

Source: Authors

2.7 CONCLUSIONS

The window of opportunity for CE that was discussed in this chapter is twofold. First, it is necessary to connect the growing demand for the localism principle and the related public and private (spatial) policy responsibility with the other CE principles. Second, it is necessary that this effective operationalisation and territorialisation of circular technologies and design and circular socio-economic and ecological policies occur at the urban and regional levels. The paradox is, however, that the current way in which CE is operationalised and territorialised at that subnational level is not yet (fully) "updated" as a result of the geopolitical "reality check" triggered by the war in Ukraine and the geopolitical turmoil. Thus, as soon as possible, planners and policymakers who are effectively working on spatial plans and policies should consider the ecological and socio-economic value of land-use functions, such as remanufacturing or waste treatment, and try to avoid the "standard", implicit course of action to externalise these functions and place them "out of sight". Thus, if we manage to put localism as a central principle of CE to enable the scales to converge (Figure 2.2), perhaps a positive answer can be given to Latour's[53] question that started this chapter. In closing, much of the reasoning in this chapter is EU oriented. That said, we believe that the window of opportunity for CE policies that we explained here is relevant for many governments and territorial administrations around the world that face similar deglobalisation challenges and wish to combine economic and ecological policy goals.

Practitioner's perspective

The Dutch government intends to achieve a fully circular economy (CE) by 2050. PBL — Netherlands Environmental Assessment Agency — supports this process with various forms of research and knowledge development. A recent study has addressed the potential spatial implications of the transition to CE, and what this means for spatial planning policy in the Netherlands.[54] In this study, we have developed four different CE scenarios in 2050. These scenarios reflect the five CE principles described in chapter 1, with "greening of production processes" added as a separate principle. The scale at which circular flows and loops operate (the extent of localism) is an important determining factor in how CE will take shape in spatial terms (e.g., how industrial zones, business sites and ports will develop, what amenities will be needed in cities and regions). Moreover, our research shows that in the transition to CE, geographical proximity matters also in other ways (in addition to localism in circular flows), as collaborations, innovations and the development of circular solutions rely on actors and activities being physically close. Finally, PBL research also highlights that moving towards a CE can contribute to strengthening the strategic autonomy of the Netherlands and Europe regarding the supply of resources.[55]

***Emil Evenhuis** is a researcher in urban and regional development at PBL — Netherlands Environmental Assessment Agency*

NOTES

1 Latour B (2022) Is Europe's soil changing beneath our feet? *Géopolitique, Réseau, Énergie, Environnement, Nature*, 2: 92–97, at 97. https://geopolitique.eu/en/articles/is-europes-soil-changing-beneath-our-feet/

2 Latour (2022), see Reference 1.

3 COM (2023) *A Green Deal Industrial Plan for the Net-Zero Age*. Brussels: European Commission. https://commission.europa.eu/strategy-and-policy/priorities-2019-2024/european-green-deal/green-deal-industrial-plan_en

4 See https://environment.ec.europa.eu/strategy/circular-economy-action-plan_en/.

5 Cf. Bourdin S, Galliano D and Gonçalves A (2021). Circularities in territories: opportunities & challenges. *European Planning Studies*, 30(7), 1183–1191. https://doi.org/10.1080/09654313.2021.1973174

6 Cf. Van den Berghe K, Tsui T, Nefs M, Iliopoulos G, Papadimitriou C, Fitzgerald T, Bonte T and Arrindell A (2024) Spatial planning of the circular economy in uncertain times: Focusing on the changing relation between port, city, and hinterland. *Maritime Transport Research*, 7: 100120. https://doi.org/10.1016/j.martra.2024.100120

7 Meadows D H, Meadows D L, Randers J and Behrens W W (1972). *The Limits to Growth: A Report to The Club of Rome (1972)*. New York: Universe Books.

8 In this perspective, see also Burger M, Stavropoulos S, Ramkumar S, Dufourmont J and van Oort F (2019) The heterogeneous skill-base of circular economy employment. *Research Policy*, 48(1): 248–261. https://doi.org/10.1016/j.respol.2018.08.015

9 Curtis F (2003) Eco-localism and sustainability. *Ecological Economics*, 46(1): 83–102. https://doi.org/10.1016/S0921-8009(03)00102-2

10 North P (2010) Eco-localisation as a progressive response to peak oil and climate change — A sympathetic critique. *Geoforum*, 41(4): 585–594. https://doi.org/10.1016/j.geoforum.2009.04.013

11 Bourdin et al. (2021), see Reference 5.

12 Krähmer K (2021) Are green cities sustainable? A degrowth critique of sustainable urban development in Copenhagen. *European Planning Studies*, 29(7): 1272–1289. https://doi.org/10.1080/09654313.2020.1841119

13 Van den Berghe K and Verhagen T (2021) Making it concrete: Analysing the role of concrete plants' locations for circular city policy goals. *Frontiers in Built Environment*, 7(136). https://doi.org/10.3389/fbuil.2021.748842

14 Latour (2022), see Reference 1.

15 Henderson J, Dicken P, Hess M, Coe N and Yeung, H W-c (2002) Global production networks and the analysis of economic development. *Review of International Political Economy*, 9(3): 436–464.

16 North (2010), see Reference 10.

17 Weber H (2022) Nazi German waste recovery and the vision of a circular economy: The case of waste paper and rags. *Business History*, 64(5): 882–903. https://doi.org/10.1080/00076791.2021.1918105

18 Sunley P (2008) Relational economic geography: A partial understanding or a new paradigm? *Economic Geography*, 84(1): 1–26. https://doi.org/10.1111/j.1944-8287.2008.tb00389.x

19 Calisto Friant M, Vermeulen W J V and Salomone R (2020) A typology of circular economy discourses: Navigating the diverse visions of a contested paradigm. *Resources, Conservation and Recycling*, 161. https://doi.org/10.1016/j.resconrec.2020.104917

20 Raworth K (2017) *Doughnut Economics: Seven Ways to Think Like a 21st-Century Economist.* Chelsea, VT: Chelsea Green.

21 Calisto Friant et al. (2020), see Reference 19.

22 Calisto Friant et al. (2020), see Reference 19.

23 Latour (2022), see Reference 1.

24 North (2010), see Reference 10.

25 Curtis (2003), see Reference 9.

26 Latour (2022), see Reference 1.

27 van Bueren E, Buizer M, Van den Berghe K, Heijkers B, Meijs L., Verhagen T, Dittrich K and Sprecher B (2022) *Perspectieven op circulaire gebiedsontwikkeling. Lessen uit de Binckhorst en andere gebiedsontwikkelingen.* Accelerating the Circular Economy Zuid-Holland (ACCEZ)

28 Bucci Ancapi F, Van den Berghe K and van Bueren E (2022) The circular built environment toolbox: A systematic literature review of policy instruments. *Journal of Cleaner Production*, 373: 133918. https://doi.org/10.1016/j.jclepro.2022.133918

29 Van Schaick J (2024) Bridging gaps with a spatial strategy for the circularity transition: Practice review from Zuid-Holland, the Netherlands. *Planning Practice & Research*: 1–25. https://doi.org/10.1080/02697459.2024.2315394

30 McDowall W, Geng Y, Huang B, Barteková E, Bleischwitz R, Türkeli S, Kemp R and Doménech T (2017) Circular economy policies in China and Europe. *Journal of Industrial Ecology*, 21(3): 651–661. https://doi.org/10.1111/jiec.12597

31 COM (2015) *Closing the Loop – An EU Action Plan for the Circular Economy.* Brussels: European Commission. http://eur-lex.europa.eu/legal-content/EN/TXT/?uri=CELEX:52015DC0614

32 OECD (2016) *Policy Guidance on Resource Efficiency.* Organisation for Economic Co-operation and Development (OECD). https://doi.org/10.1787/9789264257344-en

32 Ellen MacArthur Foundation (EMF) (2016) *The Circular Economy.* https://www.ellenmacarthurfoundation.org/circular-economy

34 Williams J (2021) *Circular Cities: A Revolution in Urban Sustainability.* Abingdon: Routledge. https://doi.org/10.4324/9780429490613

35 Bourdin et al. (2021), see Reference 5.

36 Latour (2022), see Reference 1.

37 Williams (2021), see Reference 34.

38 Van den Berghe K and Vos M (2019) Circular area design or circular area functioning? A discourse-institutional analysis of circular area developments in Amsterdam and Utrecht, The Netherlands. *Sustainability*, 11(18): 4875. https://www.mdpi.com/2071-1050/11/18/4875

39 Krähmer (2021), see Reference 12.

40 Henderson et al. (2002), see Reference 15.

41 Denkwerk (2021) *Globalanceren. Hoe Nederland kan navigeren in een regionaliserende wereld.* https://denkwerk.online/rapporten/globalanceren-juni-2021/

42 Vlaamse Overheid (2021) *Ruimterapport Vlaanderen.* https://omgeving.vlaanderen.be/nl/onderzoek-cijfers-en-geoloketten/ruimterapport-2021

43 Haezendonck E and Van den Berghe K (2020) Patterns of circular transition: What is the circular economy maturity of Belgian ports? *Sustainability*, 12(21): 9269. https://www.mdpi.com/2071-1050/12/21/9269

44 Van den Berghe K (2024) Bedrijvigheid en wonen. Van central business naar central (re)manufacturing district? In H Remoy, G van Bortel, E Heurkens and R van Venrooij (eds.), *Transformatie naar woningen*, pp. 231–242. Delft: Delft Open.

45 Bucci Ancapi F, Van den Berghe K and van Bueren E (2024) Circular city policy coherence in Greater London. *Cities*, 155: 105423. https://doi.org/10.1016/j.cities.2024.105423

46 Van den Berghe K (2023) *Het verduurzamen van bedrijventerreinen. Hou(dt) (geen) rekening met de (veranderende maatschappelijk noodzakelijke) bedrijven.* Raad voor de leefomgeving en infrastructuur. https://research.tudelft.nl/en/publications/het-verduurzamen-van-bedrijventerreinen-houdt-geen-rekening-met-d

47 COM (2022) *Science, Research and Innovation Performance of the EU 2022 – Building a Sustainable Future in Uncertain Times.* Brussels: European Commission. https://data.europa.eu/doi/10.2777/78826

48 Latour (2022), see Reference 1.

49 Cf. Van den Berghe and Verhagen (2021), see Reference 13.

50 Cf. Williams (2021), see Reference 34.

51 Cf. Williams J (2020) The role of spatial planning in transitioning to circular urban development. *Urban Geography*, 41(6): 915–919. https://doi.org/10.1080/02723638.2020.1796042

52 Yeung H W-c (2024) From regional to global and back again? A future agenda for regional evolution and (de)globalised production networks in regional studies. *Regional Studies*, 58(7), 1480–1491. https://doi.org/10.1080/00343404.2024.2316856

53 Latour (2022), see Reference 1.

54 Rood T and Evenhuis E (2023) *Ruimte voor Circulaire Economie: Verkenning van de ruimtelijke voorwaarden voor een circulaire economie.* The Hague: PBL — Netherlands Environmental Assessment Agency. https://www.pbl.nl/publicaties/ruimte-voor-circulaire-economie

55 PBL (2023) *Integrale Circulaire Economie Rapportage.* Planbureau voor de Leefomgeving (PBL). https://www.pbl.nl/publicaties/integrale-circulaire-economie-rapportage-2023

3. Towards a care-full circular economy

Federica Bono*, Wendy Wuyts* and Elmar Willems

*Co-lead authors

Keywords: care; human and non-human assemblages; social justice; inclusion

New York Compost project, New York. *Source*: Wil540 art, https://commons.wikimedia.org/wiki/File:NYC_Compost_Project.jpg

Source: Authors; graphic design by Fábio Alzate Martinez (TU Delft)

https://doi.org/10.1080/2578711X.2024.2418230

Key message

A care-full CE implies caring for carers, materials, space, time, and difference. By fostering and integrating care-full relations and processes in proposed CE projects and policies, circular cities and regions will be inherently more ecologically sustainable and socially just.

3.1 OVERVIEW

This chapter reevaluates urban and regional circular economy (CE) initiatives through the lens of care and social justice, which can be seen as either corrective or complementary to a techno-managerial or profit-oriented approach to reduce resource use and waste. It advocates for policies that emphasise human and non-human relationships and dependencies as core to sustainability. By *beginning* with care, we examine various formal and informal CE initiatives to identify existing elements of care in the management of soil, materials, waste and spatial–temporal relationships, as well as in interactions with people. Drawing on theories and practical evidence, this chapter presents recommendations for designing, implementing, and evaluating CE projects and policies that are more inclusive and attentive to the diverse needs of communities and ecosystems. We present a dashboard that invites planners and designers to *begin* the analysis with *who* is doing the care work and *what* it looks like and *how*, and the extent to which the work of care is collective and redistributed across gender, class, ethnicity or species.

3.2 INTRODUCTION

Urban and regional initiatives of circularity increasingly call for placing inclusiveness, health and social justice at their core.[1] The European Circular Cities and Regions Initiative, for example, issued a call for proposals for circular systemic solutions to increase the focus on social outcomes and human well-being and address inequalities and lack of social cohesion.[2] A recent emphasis on social outcomes and prerequisites of so-called "social CE" strategies[3] might obscure the fact that the social and socio-spatial impacts of CE have been a part of policy discussions for some time. A first reason is because CE is a new label for old practices and policies.[4,5,6,7] A second reason is that due to the recent popularisation of CE as a term, practitioners and policymakers often render it apolitical, situating it in an economic model primarily driven by a profit logic and overlooking the extensive history of practices and initiatives driven by values of social inclusivity. Critical scholars urge policymakers to depart from growth-oriented policy paradigms[8,9] and to start with social justice, putting the human foundations or needs for a good life (e.g., shelter, care) at the core of planning and policy.[10,11] This approach entails considering questions about the equal and appropriate distribution of benefits, costs, and risks at the start of policymaking and planning. Such a stance for social justice implies ethical questions and brave political decisions that are removed from the existing social and economic order in which the dominant CE discourse is embedded.

https://doi.org/10.1080/2578711X.2024.2418230

There are different definitions of CE, but the dominant interpretation relies on technocentric and ecomodernist ideals of circularity with a focus on economic and technological indicators. Current CE initiatives commodify and formalise practices of recycling, repair and reuse, exclude marginalised and informal labour,[12] or tend to neglect or stand indifferent to long and untransparent chains of production, extraction and waste treatment around the globe. At times it even appears that economic prosperity subordinates CE's goal of environmental quality, with little mention of social equity.[13,14] Within the earliest notions of CE, however, we find traces of transformative thinking and strong considerations of inclusion, social justice and democratic participation.[15] Building on these early approaches, scholars argue for the re-introduction of values that acknowledge and foreground inter-human and human–nature connections and relationships as important pillars of circular presents and futures.[16,17,18,19] Putting social justice at the centre of circular policymaking and planning is crucial both for normative reasons[20,21] and for pragmatic reasons, to avoid greenwashing and to ensure mobilisation of support and participation of citizens and relevant stakeholders.[22]

Informed by feminist insights and ethics of care,[23,24,25] we suggest that to transform economies into circular and socially just economies we need to recognise and revalue "care-relationships that are central to all ecologies and economies".[26] To *begin* with care is to recognise that it is fundamental to all economies, while doing otherwise risks not being able to reach the goal of better sustaining life and the planet. Specifically, it is important to ask "*who* is doing the care work necessary in transforming our political economies and ecologies"[27] in terms of gender, class, ethnicity and also including our non-human others,[28,29]

> *what* this care work now entails, and *how* we might — collectively, across gender and other lines of class, sexuality, culture, species — both redistribute and proliferate the work of care for the sake of human species and the rest of our planetary companions (emphasis added).[30]

We follow Tronto's definition of care as:

> a species activity that includes everything that we do to maintain, continue, and repair our 'world' so that we can live in it as well as possible. That world includes our bodies, ourselves, and our environment, all of which we seek to interweave in a complex, life-sustaining web.[31]

In the context of CE, care manifests as the cultivation of relational practices that support mutual dependence and the collective stewardship of resources.[32,33,34,35] Emphasising the interconnectedness of social, environmental and economic well-being, care is vital for social and environmental justice as it is crucial for world sustenance and repair.[36]

To *begin* with care and envision what care-full circular cities or regions could entail, there is no need to start from a blank slate. Instead, we can draw upon existing critical social science research for imagining inclusive circular cities and regions[37] and avant-garde initiatives that embody its principles. This chapter sheds light on such initiatives, underscoring that long before CE became a staple in local, national and regional policy discourses, there was already a rich body of projects pioneering the very concepts that define a social inclusive, care-full, CE today. Shifting the focus from a logic of profitability to the concept of care will help us to find interesting opportunities for policy and practice. Our main guiding question is: What does it mean to *begin* with care in a CE and how might this stimulate a more inclusive circular approach? By foregrounding care as the cornerstone of inclusive CE policies, this chapter challenges the logic of profitability in different visions of the CE and emphasises the importance of non-monetary values and relationships.

3.3 CARE-LESS REUSE, REPAIR AND RECYCLING PRACTICES

Policy practice in CE is usually centred around the "R"-strategies (i.e., recycle, reuse, reduce).[38] In what follows, we build on the literature on care and feminist political economy to highlight the shortcomings or "care-less" dimensions of those policy practices aimed at reusing, repairing and recycling.

3.3.1 Reuse

One main element of a CE is producing goods in such a way that they can be easily reused. Cities, regions and other government entities across the world set up programmes to facilitate and support the reuse of products by sponsoring community swaps, material banks for temporary storage, and other events and/or spaces.[39,40] The key for reuse is the standardisation of components and materials and this is sometimes promoted before recycling due to higher "profitability".[41] Yet, such focus on profitability implies a continuous flow of materials and, thus, unwanted goods, which raises the question of how the issue of overconsumption is tackled. Indeed, even without specific CE policies, for-profit reuse spaces such as second-hand markets and thrift stores already overflow.[42] They depend on the overconsumption in the Global North of "fast" goods (fast fashion, electronics, furniture) that are produced in unsustainable and precarious — sometimes near slavery — conditions.[43,44] Goods are given away simply because they have become undesirable rather than unusable, what Berry[45] calls a linear throwaway society.[46] The second-hand goods commodity chain extracts surplus value from — mainly — women who conduct the labour of gathering and donating goods for free and — often unpaid — volunteers who sort, process and bundle donations.[47] Next, thrift stores and charities recreate value and recommodify these unwanted goods to become either spaces for neoliberal micro-entrepreneurial "hipster" activities or lucrative commercial businesses that resell and ship items to the Global South, which is highly unsustainable from both environmental and social standpoints.[48,49] Second-hand items discarded in the North are recycled and retailed for profit in the South, reproducing unequal patterns of economic development.[50] In the North, poor or vintage re-sellers conduct precarious labour by spending hours sorting through bins filled with hazardous and unsanitary items in second-hand "outlets".[51,52] In other words, the reuse economy envelops donation dumping practices in North and South in which unpaid and "uncared-for" labour and non-human nature subsidises the extraction and accumulation of profits.

3.3.2 Repair

Just like with reuse, policymakers prioritise repair to extend life spans and reduce consumption.[53] A review of the literature reveals a primarily technocratic and apolitical view of repair as a tool for profitability and reinforcing the status quo.[54,55] A personal responsibility as part of a "sustainable consumer lifestyle" or a service offered in a corporate–consumer relationship acts in a depoliticising way, just as the promotion of repair cafes removes the issue from the political arena.[56] In those instances where labour is considered in the form of the creation of job opportunities, it is predominantly low-skilled, low-valued labour.[57] At the same time, it has become a fashionable activity in middle- and upper-class gentrified neighbourhoods.[58] Further, when promoted in an individualised and depoliticised way, repair sustains gendered divisions of labour and devalues domestic care work as instrumental for economic growth.[59] As such, if remained uncontested, repair risks sustaining unequal power relations and a greenwashing strategy for businesses.[60,61] At the same time, however, collective, community-based expressions of repair can present a political contestation against individual consumerism. Indeed, emotional attachment and care, rather than instrumentalism, are frequent motivations for repair and present opportunities for collectivisation and politicisation.[62] Beginning with care could then also lead to a disruption of traditional gender norms as grassroots repair activities defy conventional and instrumental understandings of technological skills and industrial norms.[63]

3.3.3 Recycling

CE turns waste into a resource that can be exchanged for money and value added.[64] This commodification might actually increase the production of waste, rather than reduce it.[65] Additionally, CE separates waste from its social relations, ignoring the assemblage of human and non-human ecologies. Rather than value creation via labour, value is added via processes of appropriation in highly unequal waste supply chains that depend on low-waged or non-salaried labour for collecting and sorting waste. Along the supply chain, materials are sorted, collected and inserted into the productive circuits centred around factories. This formalisation, alongside the commodification, of the waste management process risks to further marginalise informal workers and increase their dependency on corporate control.[66,67]

 https://doi.org/10.1080/2578711X.2024.2418230

As such, exploited informal workers and households *subsidise* recycling factories and plants and the accumulation of profits. Not only are there highly uneven power relations embedded in the waste supply chain, but also places of waste collection, and especially those of re-insertion of waste, are contested spaces in or outside cities, across continents worldwide. As waste becomes a commodity, we observe more clearly a hierarchy of more and less profitable activities. Even under the European Union's Waste Framework Directive, which can be regarded as a frontrunner piece of environmental legislation, rapid profit-making with higher value waste streams is perfectly possible at the expense of lower grade recycling streams that end up in precarious conditions in Africa or Asia. Indeed, common CE discourses treat as secondary implications for people and ecologies elsewhere, in favour of local or regional growth.[68]

3.4 EXAMPLES OF CARE-FULL CIRCULAR ECONOMY

In this section, we present a curated collection of case studies intended to inspire the development of care-full CE initiatives. Our selection spans both institutional and grassroots efforts, encompassing formal CE activities as well as informal practices that may not traditionally be labelled as CE. Instead of providing a comprehensive evaluation of these practices, we focus on identifying and emphasising specific principles that resonate with our definitions of care. Specifically, we have selected six case studies that vary not only geographically but also in their care assemblage of (non-)humans.[69,70,71] In other words, we *begin* the analysis with *who* is doing the care work and *what* it looks like and *how*, and the extent to which the work of care is collective and redistributed across gender, class, ethnicity or species. Table 3.1 illustrates the who, what and how of each of the six chosen cases. It is important to note that this information reflects the circumstances at the time of study by other researchers or ourselves and may not necessarily represent the current status of these initiatives. We also encourage policymakers, planners and urban designers to view this table as a sort of "dashboard" that can serve as inspiration for a tool in their policymaking arsenal. It could enable them to compile a list of initiatives within their city or region and assess whether they have achieved a diverse and effective mix of the who, what and how of care.

3.4.1 Regenerate Lebanon

Regenerate Lebanon is a pilot CE village constructed during the 17 October Revolution that took place in 2019 and 2020 in Beirut. It provides an example of a CE that allows human and non-human care. The project consisted of different solar- and bicycle-powered "tent stations" in the middle of the protests, including a zero-waste kitchen, a water refill station

Table 3.1. Overview of the case studies and the presence of care work

	Case study	Who cares?	What is cared for?	How is care distributed?
1	Regenerate Lebanon, Lebanon	Community members and volunteers, solar energy, bicycles, tents, and other supplies and equipment	People's basic needs, the environment, overall well-being	A collective of diverse community members in terms of nationality, class and political ideologies incorporating indigenous practices and cultures
2	Saitex, Vietnam	People with disabilities, Saitex, modified equipment	People with disabilities, their time, surplus materials	Community-building and valuing domestic time
3	New York City Compost Project (NYCCP), NY, USA	Diverse collective of paid, unionised and volunteer labour in combination with non-human materialities (e.g., soil, food waste, worms, microbes, garden tools, etc.)	Waste, soils, environmental labour, disadvantaged youth of colour	Community-building, redistributing the unequal environmental burden of municipal waste management, redistributing benefits to local trees and soils
4	Repurposing empty houses, Onomichi, Japan	Community organisations	Empty spaces, materials, heritage, identity	Maintaining and improving a social network of caring
5	0.666, Oostende, Belgium	Non-profits, volunteers	Polluted land, existing buildings, creativity, innovation, reflections	Supporting social well-being, education and community engagement amidst environmental remediation
6	Frauen-Werk-Stadt I, Vienna, Austria	Women, families	Time, domestic work	Gender-sensitive urban planning that incorporates care tasks into daily transport and residential design

and co-working areas, and educated people on things such as reducing waste, planting and composting. It incorporated heritage practices such as traditional methods of food preservation and connections to ancestral land-based healing. It relied on community participation, with a large number of volunteers and in-kind community contributions such as supplies and equipment. The initiative aimed to show people the root causes of corruption and poverty and promote circular solutions for economic and ecological equity.[72]

3.4.2 Saitex, Vietnam

Saitex, a textile company in Ho Chi Min, Vietnam, formed an initiative where people with disabilities are hired to recycle surplus materials from the main production line into new clothing.[73] While this approach seems to be about job creation, it also involves the appropriate adaptation of equipment, a free transportation service and short workdays to maintain work–life balance without reducing wages. Employees proudly related their ability to contribute monetarily to their family needs while at the same time finding community. The case is an example of the care for and inclusion of vulnerable communities and criticises the lack of investments of the city in diverse people's needs.

3.4.3 Community composting in New York City, United States

Founded in 1993 by the Department of Sanitation, the New York City Compost Project (NYCCP) in New York State provides technical assistance and training at community gardens and funds multiple grassroots sustainable sustainability organisations.[74] NYCCP facilitated the behavioural change, education and community outreach necessary to make composting accessible to a diversity of New Yorkers. A variety of actors, including NYCCP-trained master composters, micro- and municipal collectors of organic waste, unionised staff, paid disadvantaged youth, and volunteers in combination with non-human compost companions and different materialities work together, thereby racially and economically diversifying the sustainability movement. Community composting increases social cohesion and enhances individual and environmental well-being and non-market transactions such as compost-sharing circulate resources to where they are most needed. Decades of collective action by citizen groups and the citizens committee for New York, environmental justice and waste advocacy groups, composters, gardeners, and their city council representatives have resulted in continuous funding for community composting, availability of space, and policies that protect and incentivise these practices, despite austerity politics.[75]

3.4.4 Repurposing empty houses in Onomichi, Japan

Japan has millions of unused empty buildings. In 2014, the national authority enacted a law that gave local governments the rights and the protection to intervene in the management of empty houses. This is a departure from the previous strong national homeownership policy which stipulated that authorities could be sued by homeowners if they were to claim and/or demolish these constructions. Local governments, such as Onomichi Town, handed over the responsibility and support of managing these empty spaces and houses to community organisations, who used the circular activities of reclaiming, repurposing, and reusing as means to maintain and improve a social network of caring for materials, existing buildings, heritage and identity, and each other.[76]

3.4.5 O.666, Oostende, Belgium

In the Flemish coastal town of Oostende, O.666[77] unites about 10 different non-profits active in the field of social well-being, immigration, education, youth empowerment, arts, creativity and CE. O.666 steadily evolved as part of a city redevelopment programme in 2015. A heavily polluted piece of land ("blackfield") was appropriated by the Public Flemish Waste Agency to remediate the polluted soils. Temporary use was allowed, and different organisations found fertile ground in the buildings and the regenerated piece of land. The social-circular dimension was formulated as the core vision of everything that will be developed and promoted. It has become a space of co-creation for a more inclusive and sustainable future. Nonetheless, the initiative remains vulnerable due to the reliance on volunteers, tight working budgets, high energy prices, the uncertainty of support from the city in the mid- or long-terms, and spatial developments.

3.4.6 Frauen-Werk-Stadt I in Vienna, Austria

Frauen-Werk-Stadt I, a residential complex built in between 1995 and 1997, integrates transport planning with social service facilities (e.g., nursery, police). It fits in the decades-old tradition of Vienna to support gender via planning and include different interests and needs, especially of children.[78] The Frauen-Werk-Stadt I project was ahead of its time, prefiguring the principles that would later be embraced by Vienna's 2022 sustainable development strategy[79] and Circular Wien's 2022 advocacy for 15-minute cities.[80] Frauen-Werk-Stadt I considered the everyday space–time patterns of women who often combine their jobs with care tasks, resulting in a complex use of the transportation network. This avant-garde initiative incorporated gender-sensitive urban planning and integrated essential social services within a residential complex, mirroring the future vision of urban accessibility where every day needs — such as housing, education, work, shopping, healthcare and leisure — are met within a 15-minute radius from one's home.

3.5 KEY LEARNING POINTS FOR POLICY

The selection of cases, while geographically and demographically very different, all question the idea of profitability as the most important principle, aiming to put non-monetary values first. These different cases show how circularity planning can be seen as an opportunity not only to ascribe value to care work but also to collectivise it. High-quality social and more-than-human relationships are one of the larger pillars of a more sustainable society.[81] In what follows, we suggest five specific ways forward for a care-full CE.

3.5.1 Care for carers

To *begin* with care is to recognise and value all who do the work on which CE depends. Recognition of "the invisible heroes", or rather invisible heroic communities, is key.[82,83] Additionally, if we consider this work to be important, it should be compensated as such. Policies and programmes should consider an ethical and monetary revaluation of carers' contributions to society.[84] This not only includes considerations of salary and benefits but also ensures quality domestic well-being. Importantly, this revaluation should span across socio-economic class and also across geographies.

3.5.2 Care for materials

It is only natural for any circularity project to care for materials. But to really care implies a move away from technocratic, instrumentalist views of materials and to recognise non-humans' own active care work as well as their entanglements with social relations. As such, CE can learn from indigenous, informal, improvised or everyday practices where materials are extracted, broken down, repaired, reused, and recycled around principles of solidarity and social justice.[85,86,87]

3.5.3 Care for space

Ensuring communal access to non-market spaces, where the logic of profit is absent, is important to realise the broader social, economic and environmental goals of CE.[88] Under-used buildings or empty spaces are ideal places for long-term social-circular innovation, creativity and experimentation. Additionally, caring for space can be linked with well-being indicators (e.g., a sense of belonging, identity and the need for preserving heritage). Such contemporary commons of physical resources, knowledge or cultural practices ensure that "access, use, benefit but also responsibility and care are widely distributed".[89]

3.5.4 Care for time

In a CE, time–space relationships change in a way that it is comfortable for many with different time schedules to work, travel, and care in comfortable and resource-efficient ways. Efficient schedules and locations of public transport and services can reduce travel distances and time. Another way to increase care for time is the re-evaluation of the time horizons of projects and programmes. Despite their good intentions, short-term policy instruments often reinforce more injustices because they do not grasp the long-term political and caring work required for transformation.[90,91] A third aspect is situated in one of the key principles of circularity: slowing down loops. Caring for time means embracing slowness, which contributes to the required political and caring work for a care-full circular transition.[92]

3.5.5 Care for difference

A care-full CE builds community and emphasises the collective dimension of care. As such, it needs to be fundamentally diverse.[93,94] Starting with care allows for the possibility of multiple diverse circular economies and circular futures.[95,96] Additionally, it recognises regions, cities or neighbourhoods as assemblages of diverse human and non-human actors and values those circular practices that already exist.[97,98] Crucially, focusing on local communities as bearers of a collective vision and wisdom, rather than on what is missing or broken, allows for inclusive futures. Moving away from so-called "damage-centred work" to "desire-centred work"[99] explicitly recognises informal and marginalised carers, the spaces they inhabit and in which they work, and their everyday experiences as important actors, hubs and values for a CE-based development strategy of the city or state.

3.6 CONCLUSIONS

To begin with care is to ask who cares, what is cared for and how care is distributed. A care-full CE implies caring for carers, materials, space, time and difference. By fostering and integrating care-full relations and processes in proposed CE projects and policies, circular cities and regions will be inherently more ecologically sustainable and socially just.

Practitioner's perspective

The first focus should always be circularity, especially trying to keep resources and raw materials functional as long as possible. So we look for the longest and most optimal use of resources. But the unique thing about O.666 is that all our activities have a great social commitment. Thus, the different circular activities and the different products we make always have an aspect of co-creation with disadvantaged groups.

***Philippe Martens**, Coordinator of O.666, a testing ground for circular economy, social and corporate responsibility in Oostende, Belgium*

NOTES

1 Vanhuyse F, Rezaie S, Englund M, Jokiaho J, Henrysson M and André K (2022) Including the social in the circular: A mapping of the consequences of a circular economy transition in the city of Umeå, Sweden. *Journal of Cleaner Production*, 380: 134893. https://doi.org/10.1016/j.jclepro.2022.134893

2 European Commission (2020). *Circular economy.* https://ec.europa.eu/info/sites/default/files/research_and_innovation/green_deal/gdc_stakeholder_engagement_topic_03-2_circular_economy.pdf

3 For example, ICLEI and City of Turku (2021) *Circular Turku. A Roadmap Towards Resource Wisdom.* https://circulars.iclei.org/wp-content/uploads/2021/11/Circular-Turku-Roadmap_final_comp.pdf

4 Kovacic Z, Strand R and Völker T (2020) *The Circular Economy in Europe: Critical Perspectives on Policies and Imaginaries*. Routledge. https://www.routledge.com/The-Circular-Economy-in-Europe-Critical-Perspectives-on-Policies-and-Imaginaries/Kovacic-Strand-Volker/p/book/9781032085357

5 Korhonen J, Nuur C, Feldmann A and Birkie S E (2018) Circular economy as an essentially contested concept. *Journal of Cleaner Production*, 175: 544–552. https://doi.org/10.1016/j.jclepro.2017.12.111

6 Marin J and De Meulder B (2018) Interpreting circularity: Circular city representations concealing transition drivers. *Sustainability*, 10(5), article 5. https://doi.org/10.3390/su10051310

7 Marjanović M, Wuyts W, Marin J and Williams J (2022) Uncovering the holistic pathways to circular cities — The case of Alberta, Canada. *Highlights of Sustainability*, 1(2), article 2. https://doi.org/10.54175/hsustain1020006

8 Bassens D Kębłowski, W and Lambert D (2020) Placing cities in the circular economy: Neoliberal urbanism or spaces of socio-ecological transition? *Urban Geography*, 41(6): 893–897. https://doi.org/10.1080/02723638.2020.1788312

9 Calisto Friant M, Vermeulen W J V and Salomone R (2024) Transition to a sustainable circular society: More than just resource efficiency. *Circular Economy and Sustainability*, 4(1): 23–42. https://doi.org/10.1007/s43615-023-00272-3

10 For example, Raworth K (2018) *Doughnut Economics.* Chelsea, VT: Chelsea Green. https://www.chelseagreen.com/product/doughnut-economics-paperback/

11 For example, Schöggl J-P, Stumpf L and Baumgartner R J (2020) The narrative of sustainability and circular economy — A longitudinal review of two decades of research. *Resources, Conservation and Recycling*, 163: 105073. https://doi.org/10.1016/j.resconrec.2020.105073

12 Isenhour C and Reno J (2019) On materiality and meaning: Ethnographic engagements with reuse, repair & care. *Worldwide Waste: Journal of Interdisciplinary Studies*, 2(1): 1–8. https://doi.org/10.5334/wwwj.27

13 McLaren D, Niskanen J and Anshelm J (2020) Reconfiguring repair: Contested politics and values of repair challenge instrumental discourses found in circular economies literature. *Resources, Conservation & Recycling: X*, 8: 100046. https://doi.org/10.1016/j.rcrx.2020.100046

14 Vanhuyse F, Fejzić E, Ddiba D and Henrysson M (2021) The lack of social impact considerations in transitioning towards urban circular economies: A scoping review. *Sustainable Cities and Society*, 75: 103394. https://doi.org/10.1016/j.scs.2021.103394

15 Calisto Friant M (2020, December 16) The circular economy: Transformative vision or oxymoronic illusion? *Circular Conversations.* https://www.circularconversations.com/research-series-young-researchers/the-circular-economy-transformative-vision-or-oxymoronic-illusion

16 Clube R K M and Tennant M (2022) Social inclusion and the circular economy: The case of a fashion textiles manufacturer in Vietnam. *Business Strategy & Development*, 5(1): 4–16. https://doi.org/10.1002/bsd2.179

17 Genovese A and Pansera M (2021) The circular economy at a crossroads: Technocratic eco-modernism or convivial technology for social revolution? *Capitalism Nature Socialism*, 32(2): 95–113. https://doi.org/10.1080/10455752.2020.1763414

18 Jaeger-Erben M, Jensen C, Hofmann F and Zwiers J (2021) There is no sustainable circular economy without a circular society. *Resources, Conservation and Recycling*, 168: 105476. https://doi.org/10.1016/j.resconrec.2021.105476

19 James P (2022) Re-embedding the circular economy in circles of social life: Beyond the self-repairing (and still-rapacious) economy. *Local Environment*, 27(10–11): 1208–1224. https://doi.org/10.1080/13549839.2022.2040469

20 Moreau V, Sahakian M, van Griethuysen P and Vuille F (2017) Coming full circle: Why social and institutional dimensions matter for the circular economy. *Journal of Industrial Ecology*, 21(3): 497–506. https://doi.org/10.1111/jiec.12598

21 Wuyts W and Marin J (2022) "Nobody" matters in circular landscapes. *Local Environment*, 27(10–11): 1254–1271. https://doi.org/10.1080/13549839.2022.2040465

22 Niskanen J, Anshelm J and McLaren D (2020) Local conflicts and national consensus: The strange case of circular economy in Sweden. *Journal of Cleaner Production*, 261: 121117. https://doi.org/10.1016/j.jclepro.2020.121117

23 Puig de la Bellacasa M (2017) *Matters of Care*. Minneapolis: University of Minnesota Press. https://www.upress.umn.edu/9781517900656/matters-of-care/

24 Power E R (2019) Assembling the capacity to care: Caring-with precarious housing. *Transactions of the Institute of British Geographers*, 44(4): 763–777. https://doi.org/10.1111/tran.12306

25 Williams M J (2017) Care-full justice in the city. *Antipode*, 49(3): 821–839. https://doi.org/10.1111/anti.12279

26 Dombroski K, Healy S and McKinnon K (2018) Care-full community economies. In C Bauhardt and W Harcourt (eds.), *Feminist Political Ecology and the Economics of Care*, pp. 99–115. Routledge.

27 Dombroski et al. (2018), see Reference 26.

28 Puig de la Bellacasa (2017), see Reference 23.

29 Wuyts W (2024) The weed, asbestos pipe and disposable tree: Unmuting multispecies Flemish and Norwegian circular site stories for diverse circular economies. *Cambridge Journal of Regions, Economy and Society*, rsae009. https://doi.org/10.1093/cjres/rsae009

30 Dombroski et al. (2018), see Reference 26.

31 Tronto J (2020) *Moral Boundaries: A Political Argument for an Ethic of Care*. Routledge. https://doi.org/10.4324/9781003070672

32 Calisto Friant et al. (2024), see Reference 9.

33 Wuyts (2024), see Reference 29.

34 Pla-Julián I and Guevara S (2019) Is circular economy the key to transitioning towards sustainable development? Challenges from the perspective of care ethics. *Futures*, 105: 67–77. https://doi.org/10.1016/j.futures.2018.09.001

35 Hobson K and Lync N (2016) Diversifying and de-growing the circular economy: Radical social transformation in a resource-scarce world. *Futures*, 82: 15–25. https://doi.org/10.1016/j.futures.2016.05.012

36 Tronto (2020), see Reference 31.

37 Wuyts W (2024) Imagining inclusive circular cities: The role of social fiction in planning education. *Planning Practice & Research*. https://doi.org/10.1080/02697459.2024.2324235

38 Reike D, Vermeulen W J V and Witjes S (2018) The circular economy: New or refurbished as CE 3.0? – Exploring controversies in the conceptualization of the circular economy through a focus on history and resource value retention options. *Resources, Conservation and Recycling*, 135: 246–264. https://doi.org/10.1016/j.resconrec.2017.08.027

39 Marin J, Alaerts L and Van Acker K (2020) A materials bank for circular Leuven: How to monitor "Messy" circular city transition projects. *Sustainability*, 12(24), article 24. https://doi.org/10.3390/su122410351

40 Asker Kommune (2021) *Temaplan for handling mot klimaendringene* [Theme Plan for Action Against Climate Change]. Asker Kommune. https://www.asker.kommune.no/om-asker-kommune/styring-og-verdier/temaplaner-for-asker-kommune/temaplan-handling-mot-klimaendringene/

41 Stahel W (2010) Durability, function and performance. In T Cooper (ed.), *Longer Lasting Products*. Abingdon: Routledge.

42 Ayres J (2019) The work of shopping: Resellers and the informal economy at the goodwill bins. *Business History*, 61(1): 122–154. https://doi.org/10.1080/00076791.2017.1369962

43 Ayres (2019), see Reference 42.

44 Houston L and Jackson S J (2016) Caring for the "next billion" mobile handsets: Opening proprietary closures through the work of repair. *Proceedings of the Eighth International Conference on Information and Communication Technologies and Development*: 1–11. https://doi.org/10.1145/2909609.2909658

45 Berry B (2022) Glut: Affective labor and the burden of abundance in secondhand economies. *Anthropology of Work Review*, 43(1): 26–37. https://doi.org/10.1111/awr.12233

46 Ayres (2019), see Reference 42.

47 Gravestock K E (2018) *Doing good? Thrift stores and second-hand clothing donations in Victoria, BC*. University of Victoria. http://hdl.handle.net/1828/9307

48 Gravestock (2018), see Reference 47.

49 Scott M (2017) "Hipster capitalism" in the age of austerity? Polanyi meets Bourdieu's New Petite Bourgeoisie. *Cultural Sociology*, 11(1), 60–76. https://doi.org/10.1177/1749975516681226

50 For example, Brooks A (2013). Stretching global production networks: The international second-hand clothing trade. *Geoforum*, 44: 10–22. https://doi.org/10.1016/j.geoforum.2012.06.004

51 Ayres (2019), see Reference 42.

52 Berry (2022), see Reference 45.

53 McLaren et al. (2020), see Reference 13.

54 Isenhour and Reno (2019), see Reference 12.

55 McLaren et al. (2020), see Reference 13.

56 McLaren et al. (2020), see Reference 13.

57 McLaren et al. (2020), see Reference 13.

58 Savini F (2019) The economy that runs on waste: Accumulation in the circular city. *Journal of Environmental Policy & Planning*, 21(6): 675–691. https://doi.org/10.1080/1523908X.2019.1670048

59 McLaren et al. (2020), see Reference 13.
60 McLaren et al. (2020), see Reference 13.
61 Savini (2019), see Reference 58.
62 Meißner M (2021) Repair is care? – Dimensions of care within collaborative practices in repair cafes. *Journal of Cleaner Production*, 299: 126913. https://doi.org/10.1016/j.jclepro.2021.126913
63 Young M and Rosner D K (2019) Repair for the masses? Gender and care work in the fixers' collective. In I Strebel, A Bovet and P Sormani (eds.), *Repair Work Ethnographies: Revisiting Breakdown, Relocating Materiality*, pp. 313–334. Springer Nature. https://doi.org/10.1007/978-981-13-2110-8_11
64 Millington N, Stokes K and Lawhon M (2022) Whose value lies in the urban mine? Reconfiguring permissions, work, and the benefits of waste in South Africa. *Annals of the American Association of Geographers*, 112(7): 1942–1957. https://doi.org/10.1080/24694452.2022.2042181
65 Makov T and Font Vivanco D (2018) Does the circular economy grow the pie? The case of rebound effects from smartphone reuse. *Frontiers in Energy Research*, 6. https://doi.org/10.3389/fenrg.2018.00039
66 Isenhour and Reno (2019), see Reference 12.
67 McLaren et al. (2020), see Reference 13.
68 McLaren et al. (2020), see Reference 13.
69 Naylor L (2024) Diverse economies of care-full healthcare: Banking and sharing human milk. In D Primrose, R Chang and R Loeppky (eds.), *The Routledge Handbook of the Political Economy of Health and Healthcare*, pp. 459–470. Abingdon: Routledge.
70 Puig de la Bellacasa (2017), see Reference 23.
71 Wuyts (2024), see Reference 29.
72 Rosenbaum R A and Kehdy J F (2022) Cultivating circular economies in the gaps of governance: Lessons from Lebanon's ecosystem of CE micro projects. *Local Environment*, 27(10–11): 1304–1320. https://doi.org/10.1080/13549839.2022.2040466
73 Clube and Tennant (2022), see Reference 16.
74 Scott (2017), see Reference 49.
75 Morrow O and Davies A (2022) Creating careful circularities: Community composting in New York City. *Transactions of the Institute of British Geographers*, 47(2): 529–546. https://doi.org/10.1111/tran.12523
76 Wuyts W and Marjanović M (2023) The development of spatial circularity discourse in Japan: Ecomodernist, territorialised, or both? The story of Onomichi's wastescapes. *Circular Economy and Sustainability*, 3(3): 1649–1675. https://doi.org/10.1007/s43615-021-00146-6
77 O.666 (n.d.) *O.666 — Proeftuin voor circulaire economie* [O.666 — Testing Ground for Circular Economy]. https://web.o666.be/
78 Pamer V (2019) Urban planning in the most liveable city: Vienna. *Urban Research & Practice*, 12(3): 285–295.
79 City of Vienna (n.d.) *Alltags- und Frauengerechtes Planen und Bauen* [Planning and Housing Suitable for Everyday Life and for Women]. https://www.wien.gv.at/stadtentwicklung/alltagundfrauen/wohnbau.html

80 City of Vienna (2022) *Circular Wien*. http://www.circular.wien/scwr_klima_2022_web-EN.pdf
81 Morrow and Davies (2022), see Reference 75.
82 Wuyts and Marin (2022), see Reference 21.
83 Amorim de Oliveira Í (2021) Environmental justice and circular economy: Analyzing justice for waste pickers in upcoming circular economy in Fortaleza, Brazil. *Circular Economy and Sustainability*, 1(3): 815–834. https://doi.org/10.1007/s43615-021-00045-w
84 Pla-Julián and Guevara (2019), see Reference 34.
85 McLaren et al. (2020), see Reference 13.
86 Houston and Jackson (2016), see Reference 44.
87 Eriksen T H and Schober E (2017) Waste and the superfluous: An introduction. *Social Anthropology*, 25(3): 282–287. https://doi.org/10.1111/1469-8676.12422
88 Morrow O and Davies A (2022). Creating careful circularities: Community composting in New York City. *Transactions of the Institute of British Geographers*, 47(2): 529–546. https://doi.org/10.1111/tran.12523
89 Dombroski et al. (2018), see Reference 26.
90 Luger J, Kotsila P and Anguelovski I (2023) The notion of justice in funded research on urban sustainability: Performing on a postpolitical stage or staging the political? *Local Environment*, 28(1): 8–30. https://doi.org/10.1080/13549839.2022.2113867
91 Selliah S, Povilaityte-Petri V and Wuyts W (2022) Tensions and invisible costs in co-creating nature-based health knowledge in Brussels. *Urban Science*, 6(4), article 4. https://doi.org/10.3390/urbansci6040068
92 Rosenbaum and Kehdy (2022), see Reference 72.
93 Wuyts (2024), see Reference 29.
94 Hobson and Lynch (2016), see Reference 35.
95 For example, McLaren et al. (2020), see Reference 13.
96 For example, Wuyts (2024), see Reference 29.
97 Wuyts (2024), see Reference 29.
98 Escobar A (2020) *Pluriversal Politics: The Real and the Possible*. Durham: Duke University Press.
99 Tuck E (2009) Suspending damage: A letter to communities. *Harvard Educational Review*, 79(3): 409–428. https://doi.org/10.17763/haer.79.3.n0016675661t3n15

4. Implementing the circular bioeconomy in metropolitan regions

Joanna Williams

Keywords: Bioeconomy, circular, regional systems, regional planning

Supertree Grove, Singapore. *Source*: Annie Spratt, https://unsplash.com/photos/gardens-by-the-bay-singapore-McM5BW4jQHc

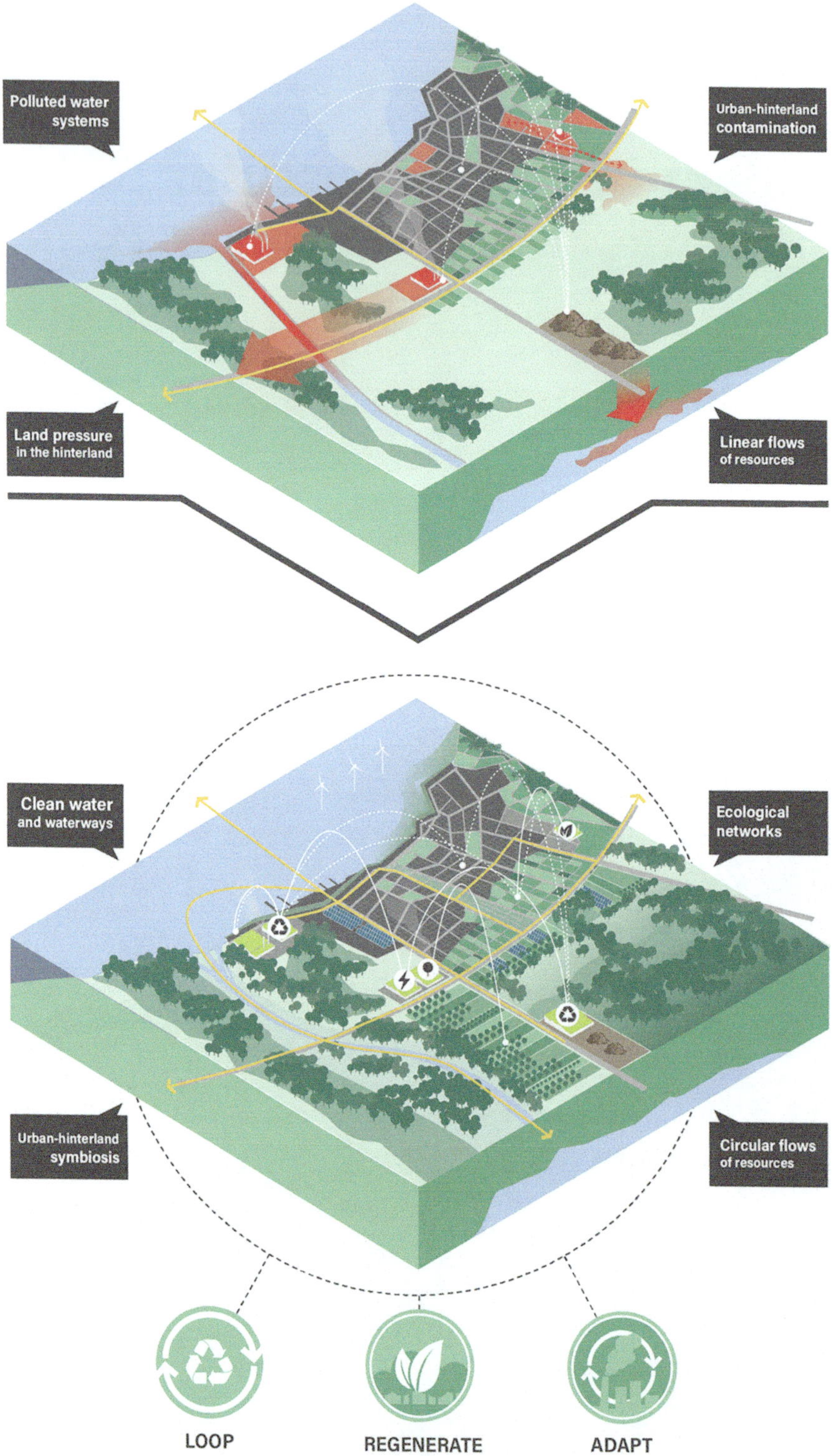

Source: Author; graphic design by Fábio Alzate Martinez (TU Delft)

Key message

A policy framework, supported by suitable institutions and policy instruments, is needed to enable a shift towards more ecologically healthy, resource sufficient, metropolitan regions.

4.1 OVERVIEW

Urban systems are consuming resources and ecosystems services beyond the global carrying capacity, which results in the liquidation of natural capital, resource shortages (particularly water, food and energy) and the degradation of urban ecosystems. A shift towards a circular bioeconomy in urban systems could help to alleviate some of these problems. In this chapter we investigate this proposition and present European examples. We explore the potential levers for transformation and role of spatial planning in this process. Finally, we assess the challenges to implementation at a city-regional scale.

4.2 INTRODUCTION

> We are using 50% more resources than the Earth can provide. By 2030, even two planets will not be enough.[1]

Urban systems are consuming resources and ecosystems services beyond the global carrying capacity,[2] which results in the liquidation of natural capital, resource shortages (particularly water, food and energy[3,4]) and the degradation of urban ecosystems.[5] A shift towards a circular bioeconomy in urban systems could help to alleviate some of these problems.[6] A circular bioeconomy valorises organic waste, renewable resources and ecosystem services. It is different from circular economy (CE), which only focuses on valorising organic waste.

Cities generate 1.3 billion tonnes of solid waste annually, a figure expected to double by 2025.[7] Approximately 50% of all resources wasted are organic. Urban biowaste and wastewater sludge are precious feedstocks for producing valuable biobased products such as food, fertilisers, chemicals, plastics and energy.[8] A circular bioeconomy can increase access to food water and energy.

Urban food production, biowaste valorisation and green infrastructure are critical for a circular bioeconomy, enabling synergies and the cyclical movement of resources and energy. These synergies create a robust and resilient urban ecology.[9,10] Put together within a complex chain of relationships green infrastructure delivers ecosystem services, which enhance biowaste recovery, and urban agriculture, and vice versa. Limiting wastewater and biowaste in an urban system reduces water pollution (particularly from sewage overspills) and soil contamination; eutrophication, loss of habitats and biodiversity; and greenhouse gas emissions. It also increases the potential for improvement in soil quality, vegetation health and biodiversity.

The 2018 updated European Bioeconomy Strategy[11] stated that cities should become circular bioeconomy hubs, producing very significant economic and environmental gains within urban systems. However, the spatial context in which urban circular bioeconomies can successfully emerge is less discussed, as are the infrastructure and services needed to support them.[12]

The governance and planning of urban circular bioeconomies has not been widely debated in the literature. Importantly, organic resource flows and related ecosystem services are not constrained by administrative boundaries. Thus, planners and policymakers need to determine the appropriate scale at which to do this, considering the intrinsic link between cities and their hinterlands when considering organic "waste", nutrient flows and ecosystem service provision. However, it is likely that existing institutional arrangements, powers and resources available to subnational bodies implementing these policies at a city-regional level are likely to be currently insufficient.[13]

4.3 BRIEF OVERVIEW OF HOW THE PROBLEM HAS BEEN TACKLED IN ACADEMIC AND POLICY RESEARCH

There has been increasing interest in the academic literature in bioeconomies, circular bioeconomies and urban bioeconomies since 2010, of which less than 1% of papers have considered the spatial aspects of delivery;[14] the role spatial planning can play in the implementation of a circular bioeconomy; and the influence policy and governance have in the transition process and in avoiding land use conflicts are less discussed.[15]

The food–water–energy nexus[16] literature provides some insights into the potential problems faced when governing an urban circular bioeconomy.[17] Urban infrastructure systems for energy, water, food and waste often operate independently, making integrated management difficult. Thus, many public, community and private actors are involved in the implementation of nexus solutions, which require governments to navigate complex power relations and governance structures. In addition, managing the interdependencies between water, energy and food systems can be technically and logistically challenging, especially in the context of rapid urbanisation, which increases demand for resources, complicating resource management efforts. These challenges highlight the need for coordinated and innovative urban governance strategies.[18]

Spatial planning could play a crucial role in promoting a circular bioeconomy by addressing various spatial and land-use challenges.[19] Spatial planning helps manage land use efficiently, ensuring that agricultural, industrial and urban development are balanced. This can prevent over-exploitation of natural resources, the degradation of ecosystem services and promote the closure of resource loops.[20] By designating protected areas and promoting green infrastructure, spatial planning also helps to preserve biodiversity and

 https://doi.org/10.1080/2578711X.2024.2418233

ecosystem services.[21,22] This is essential for maintaining the ecological balance necessary for a circular bioeconomy.[23]

Spatial planning provides frameworks for resolving land-use conflicts, such as those between agricultural production and conservation efforts;[24] or activities valorising organic waste and protecting urban green space from profitable commercial and residential development.[25,26] This ensures that different low-value, circular bioeconomic activities (e.g., anaerobic digestion, urban farming, composting facilities, etc.) are given space in overcrowded urban areas. Spatial planning can also be used to encourage decentralised biowaste management and co-location strategies, which enhance resource efficiency, reduce costs and improve sustainability.[27,28]

Spatial planning can involve stakeholders in decision-making processes, ensuring that the transition to a circular bioeconomy is inclusive and considers the needs and values of local communities.[29,30,31] It can integrate various policies related to environmental protection, economic development and social equity. This holistic approach ensures that circular bioeconomy strategies are aligned with broader sustainable development goals.[32]

However, the challenges to and levers for implementing a localised circular bioeconomy in a city-region are not properly addressed in the literature or in policy practice. Yet, this is important because natural cycles operate at this scale. There is also greater potential for public engagement in resource management and ecological regeneration at a regional scale, where the positive impacts can be seen directly. In this chapter we will investigate this dimension further.

4.4 BRIEF OVERVIEW OF HOW THE PROBLEM HAS BEEN TACKLED IN PRACTICE

An increasing number of cities (e.g., Paris, Amsterdam, London, Brussels, Stockholm) and regions in Europe (e.g., Flanders, Tampere, Lombardy) have adopted CE strategies.[33,34,35,36] There is a great deal of diversity in approach, ranging from socio-ecological to techno-economic solutions.[37] The strategies that emerge reflect the local conditions and political priorities. Subnationally many strategies focus on how to support circular businesses in cities rather than creating circular urban systems for energy, food, and water provision. A few city-regions are aiming to create circular urban bioeconomic systems.

4.4.1 Amsterdam, the Netherlands

Amsterdam aims to create a city-regional circular bioeconomy. This is hoped to be achieved through the recycling, reprocessing and energy recovery from organic waste and wastewater, to produce bioproducts (food, feedstock, construction materials, bioplastics, chemicals and pharmaceuticals) and bioenergy.[38] Interest in creating a circular bioeconomy in Amsterdam has been driven by the need for the Netherlands to become less reliant on imports of food and energy; tackle the waste of resources and reduce emissions; and become a leader in a new growing economy.

Amsterdam recycles phosphate from sewage to use as fertiliser at scale. It produces enough to fertilise the land equivalent of 10,000 football pitches annually. Other resources are being harvested from wastewater. Alginic acid is processed from granular sludge and used in the pharmaceutical and food industries. Biogas (for cooking, electricity and heat), fuels and advanced chemicals are also produced from sludge. Cellulose fibres, from toilet paper, have been used to produce building materials, paper products and bioplastics. The Power-to-Protein Project[39] extracts ammonia from sewage to create high-value proteins, sufficient to provide all the residents of Amsterdam with 35% of their primary protein requirement.

Amsterdam's existing infrastructure, its location on global trading routes and expertise in bioindustries is integral to the success of a circular bioeconomy. The city's CE strategy and the national policy framework, which support the growth of CE, provide ample political support for the venture. National and local funding support has also provided motivation for local actors to become innovators in this field.

Spatial planning has been used to support the development of the bio-cluster in the Port of Amsterdam. The bio-cluster is built on land owned and provided by the city. There is infrastructure for storing and distributing biofuel from the port. There is a direct kerosene pipeline to Schiphol International Airport and a steam pipeline that links the biodiesel plant to several sites in Amsterdam. Thus, the activities surrounding the port will use the bioenergy produced, lowering the costs of distribution. Meanwhile the green infrastructure in the city and agricultural lands outside of the city's boundary produce feedstock for the bioeconomy (alongside wastewater). Both also use the fertilisers produced. Organic resource flows are enabled and monitored by the circular resource monitor (resource flow database).[40]

4.4.2 Paris, France

Paris is also in the process of creating a city-regional circular bioeconomy.[41] This is an ambition largely driven by socio-ecological goals including: addressing waste, greenhouse gas emissions, climate adaptation, and provision of affordable food and energy. It differs from the approach in Amsterdam, which is really focused on the emergence of a new economy and economic growth.

Paris aims to create a localised food-loop within the metropolitan region. This involves the local production of food as well as reuse of food "waste". The Parisculteurs[42] initiative incentivises building and landowners in the city to allow space to be used for urban farming. This is supplemented by food production on municipally owned land surrounding Paris.

Food reuse is also crucial to closing the metropolitan food-loop. French food-reuse legislation, which requires markets and supermarkets to reuse in-date food waste, has encouraged the proliferation of food reuse schemes across the Parisienne metropolitan region by profit and not-for-profit businesses, charities and public services. This has been supported by local public funding. The remaining food waste is composted within the metro-region or converted to biogas to heat the city.

The regional, urban and related plans plan support the allocation of space in the city for green infrastructure, anaerobic digestion plants and sites for composting.[43] Temporary planning permissions have also been used to increase the coverage of green infrastructure, albeit temporarily. This has been further facilitated by a database of available sites and crowdfunding for a variety of projects. The Parisian CE strategy was produced through a highly collaborative process, which has also helped to engage key actors across the region in implementation.

This approach increases the region's food and energy security. It also helps to regenerate the local ecosystem by reducing emissions from organic waste and food miles; improving local soil quality; and increasing the green infrastructure across the city, which in turn increases climate resilience to drought and flooding It also offers the possibility of accessing affordable food and energy, adding a social solidarity dimension.[44]

4.4.3 Stockholm, Sweden

Stockholm was the first city to develop a circular system focused on energy recovery, called Ecocycles.[45,46] It was developed to increase energy security and reduce waste being sent to landfill. Sewage sludge, waste heat and refuse are used to produce energy. The heat produced from the process of purifying wastewater is used by the thermal power station. The biogas generated from the bio-digestion of sewage is used for cooking and to power the public transport system. Refuse is burnt to provide heating for homes and businesses. Ecocycles expanded to incorporate the seaport areas in the metropolitan region. Here organic waste from ships was collected and used to produce fertiliser and biogas. This also benefited the marine ecosystem, which had previously been polluted by the organic waste being dumped from ships.

Ecocycles operates throughout the Stockholm metropolitan region. Waste-water treatment plants, combined heat and power (CHP) stations, recycling, and composting facilities, alongside the users of the end-products (households, public transport services, local farmers, green infrastructure providers), are all key components of the system, which requires the provision of space and infrastructure. Ecocycles has reduced waste going to landfill by 90%. It also provides a cleaner, more secure and affordable alternative to fossil fuels for mobility, electricity and space heating. Thus, it has reduced CO_2 emissions by 29–37% and water consumption by 41–46%.[47] It has also helped to improve nutrient cycles and ensured that nutrients are provided where they are needed, rather than in water bodies, where they cause eutrophication and a loss of biodiversity.

Spatial planning is used to support Ecocycles through: the provision of compatible infrastructure (thermal power plants, anaerobic digestion facilities, provision of public transport services); the requirement for the connection of new development to the district heating system; and maintaining mixed-use, high-density and medium-rise development which supports the system.[48,49] A collaborative approach has helped to build capacity amongst developers and service providers (energy, waste, water and transport) to support Ecocycles through the infrastructure and services they provide. Conditions have been placed on new developments for urban systems to move up the waste and energy hierarchies (moving towards renewable energy, recycling and reuse of material waste), which has been supported through capacity-building activities organised by the local government and planning departments.[50,51]

4.5 CHALLENGES FOR CIRCULAR BIOECONOMIES IN CITY-REGIONS

Organic resource flows and ecosystem services operate across the administrative boundaries of cities. Thus, strategic approaches to the creation of systems underpinning a local circular bioeconomy must also go beyond these boundaries. The literature has identified many challenges to implementing circular urban systems.[52,53,54] However, there are likely to be additional challenges when implementing circular bioeconomies at a city-regional scale, as discussed below.

4.6 LACK OF INSTITUTIONAL COMPETENCIES AND RESOURCES FOR METROPOLITAN PLANNING

Cities (as clearly defined administrative jurisdictions) have competencies and resources that can be used to leverage circular urban systems (Figure 4.1). However, there are limited institutional structures operating at the metropolitan scale and the policy framework is lacking. The competencies (regulative, provisioning, capacity-building) and resources (e.g., land, finance) needed to implement circular bioeconomic systems are absent or limited. Thus, there is a lack of leverage for implementation.

In this situation, implementation is dependent on the levers available within local administrative boundaries or at a national scale. Difficulties in coordinating approaches (policies

https://doi.org/10.1080/2578711X.2024.2418233

Figure 4.1 Levers for circular development

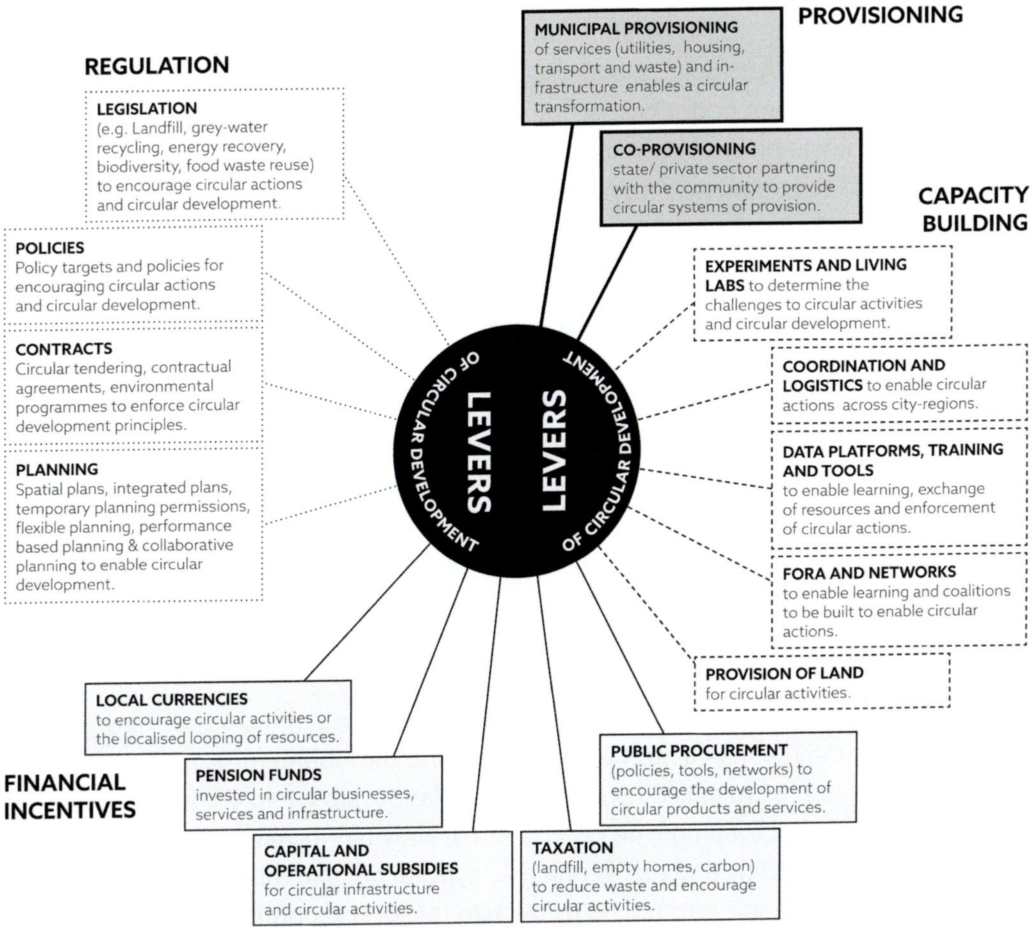

Source: Williams (2021)[55]

and levers) across local administrative boundaries are likely to arise at a metropolitan scale, which creates challenges in coordinating and planning organic resource flows[56] and ecosystem service provision cross-boundary.[57] These problems of coordination might be overcome through the creation of new institutions at a metropolitan level with a responsibility for governing resource management and ecosystem services. Such a strategy could be implemented through a metropolitan plan.

However, in the absence of new metropolitan institutions, national regulatory frameworks to support circular bioeconomic systems (e.g., national regulation in France which requires the reuse of "waste" food), resource management and the restoration of ecosystem services could enable a more coordinated approach at a metropolitan scale. The ownership of assets across local boundaries (e.g., land) may also help to leverage change at a metropolitan level (e.g., the Île-de-France region owning land in Paris's urban periphery).

4.7 THE UNEQUAL DISTRIBUTION OF DIS/BENEFITS

The scale (and locale) at which benefits/disbenefits emerge from adopting a circular bio-economy will affect both its political and social acceptance. Without a transparent cost–benefit analysis of development options, negotiating cross-border collaboration is likely to be difficult.[58] Thus, it will be important to understand the spatial distribution of benefits and disbenefits across the metro-region in order to obtain community and political support for this approach.

Such a negotiation lends itself to a more collaborative approach to cross-border, metro-planning which engages with community actors. A collaborative approach to planning at a metro-scale will also increase community awareness of options, highlighting the benefits and disbenefits of each option and thus increasing local support for the schemes chosen. Engaging the communities — through physical and online participatory activities involving the co-creation of knowledge and co-design of spatial strategies and interventions — is also likely to produce context-appropriate solutions.

4.8 SYNERGIES AND CONFLICTS WITH EXISTING URBAN POLICIES

There is also a lack of consideration of the synergies and conflicts that may emerge between regenerative, circular strategies and existing development strategies in metro-regions.[59] For example, there is a strong positive relationship between flows-localisation strategies and resource looping. The localisation of activities increases the economic feasibility of reusing, recycling and recovering energy from organic waste; reduces emissions from associated transportation; and helps to build the local economy.[60] This is one reason why Amsterdam and Paris are both taking a metropolitan approach to dealing with organic waste.[61]

There are also conflicts. For example, localisation strategies may restrict opportunities for resource looping, if there are limited producers and consumers of "waste" products within a metro-region. For example, Stockholm now imports organic waste to operate Ecocycles. Equally there are potential clashes between circular, efficiency and substitution strategies. In Stockholm, energy recovery undermines other plans to increase the municipal reuse and recycling capability as well as the move towards greater use of renewable energy (i.e., substitution). Ecocycles relies on the production of "waste", which also conflicts with efficiency strategies that remove waste.[62]

At a metropolitan scale this is further complicated by the diversity of policy and development strategies which may already be operating across different administrative areas. Again, a cross-boundary, coordinated policy response, which considers the interaction of the circular policies (looping, ecological regeneration and adaptation) with existing development policies, will be needed.

4.9 SILOED THINKING IN POLICYMAKING LEADING TO SUBOPTIMAL STRATEGIES

Currently, siloed thinking in policymaking does not support and enhance the synergies that exist between resource looping, adaptation and ecological regeneration (Figure 4.2), which emerge from adopting a circular bioeconomic system. Thus, they are likely to operate suboptimally. For instance, in Amsterdam, the recycling of residual nutrients in sewage provides food protein. This is a looping action that reduces the space needed to grow feedstock. It may also benefit the local ecosystem by reducing both soil and water pollution caused by additional nitrogen entering the water supply (ecological regeneration). If the land for feedstock is replaced by food produced for local consumers, by using regenerative practices it would also increase local food security (increasing adaptive capacity). Supporting these synergies will have implications for planning land-use activities and strategic infrastructure in metro-regions. Thus, opportunities for supporting these synergies need to be factored into decision-making, policymaking and plans across metro-regions.

4.10 LACK OF DATA FOR METROPOLITAN RESOURCE AND ECOSYSTEM SERVICE MANAGEMENT

Circular urban systems offer a range of benefits across a variety of scales.[63] However, there is no systematic appraisal as to the scale at which benefits or disbenefits arise, which might allow for a better understanding of land-use trade-offs across the metropolitan region. There is also a lack of data to provide an evidence base for these decisions (see chapter 5).

Data are essential for policymakers to determine the best development options and to monitor progress. However, collecting comprehensive, consistent, useful data for urban systems is a major challenge. Issues around ownership, privacy and commercial competitiveness restrict access to data.[64] The quality of the data produced is also problematic due to limited coverage, inconsistent monitoring and frameworks.[65,66]

More specifically, there are limited data for monitoring ecosystem services in urban and regional systems.[67,68] Similar problems exist for monitoring the flows and stocks of resources and energy through urban systems. These data are needed to understand and optimise

Figure 4.2 Synergistic benefits from adopting a circular development pathway

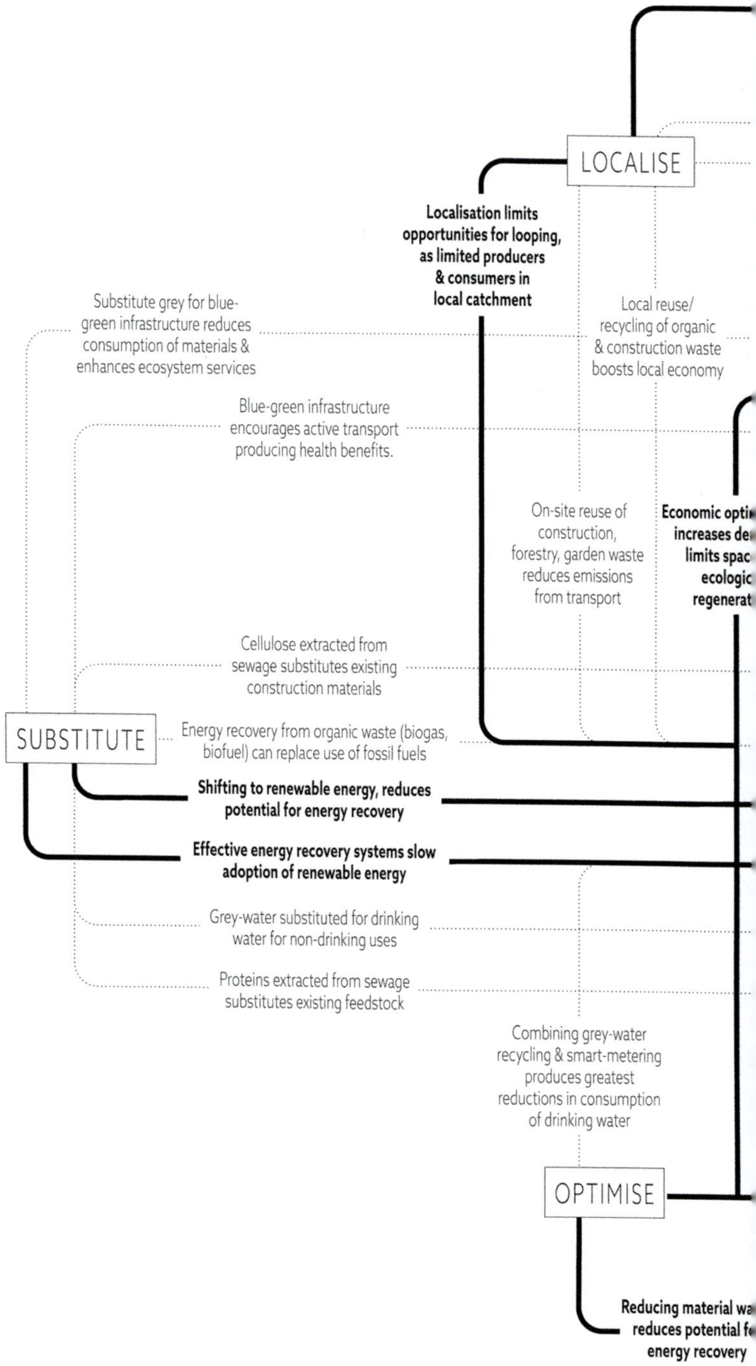

Source: Williams (2021)[69]

https://doi.org/10.1080/2578711X.2024.2418233

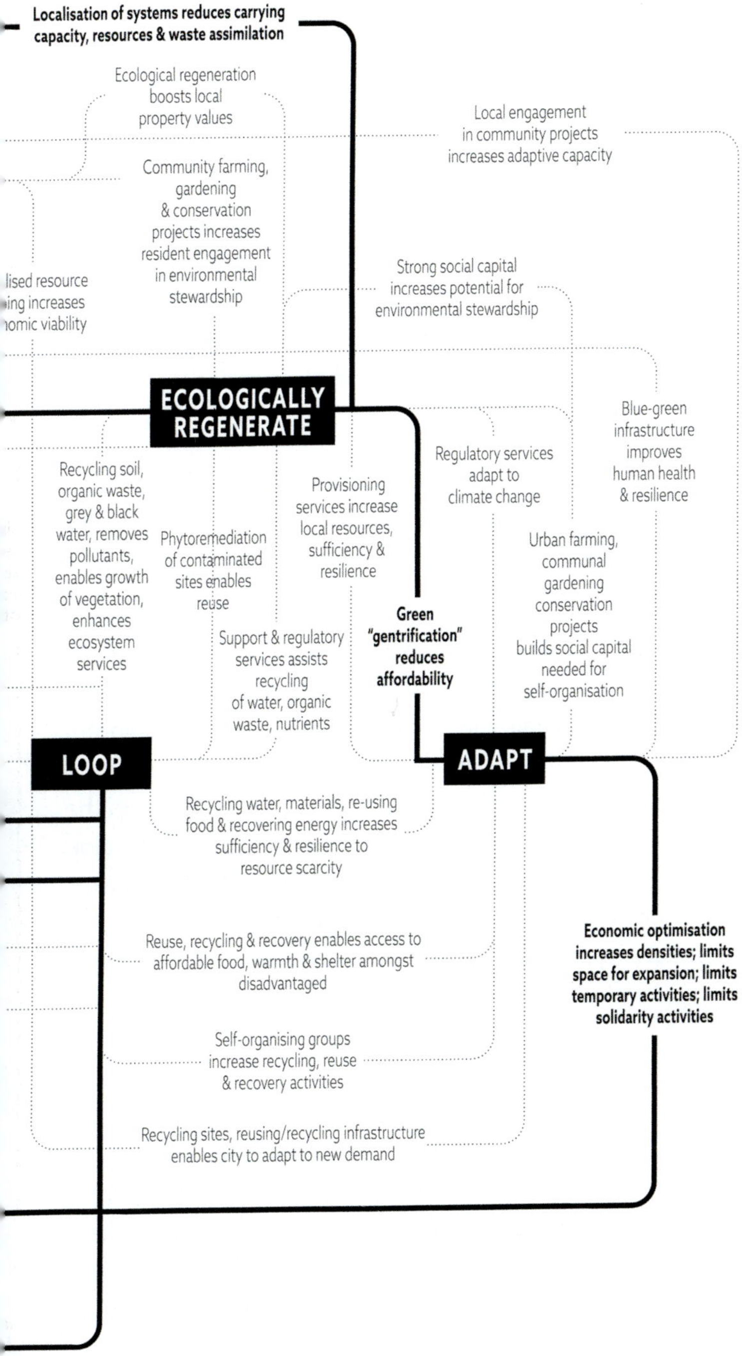
Localisation of systems reduces carrying capacity, resources & waste assimilation
Ecological regeneration boosts local property values
Local engagement in community projects increases adaptive capacity
Community farming, gardening & conservation projects increases resident engagement in environmental stewardship
lised resource
ing increases
omic viability
Strong social capital increases potential for environmental stewardship
ECOLOGICALLY REGENERATE
Blue-green infrastructure improves human health & resilience
Regulatory services adapt to climate change
Recycling soil, organic waste, grey & black water, removes pollutants, enables growth of vegetation, enhances ecosystem services
Phytoremediation of contaminated sites enables reuse
Provisioning services increase local resources, sufficiency & resilience
Urban farming, communal gardening conservation projects builds social capital needed for self-organisation
Green "gentrification" reduces affordability
Support & regulatory services assists recycling of water, organic waste, nutrients
LOOP
ADAPT
Recycling water, materials, re-using food & recovering energy increases sufficiency & resilience to resource scarcity
Economic optimisation increases densities; limits space for expansion; limits temporary activities; limits solidarity activities
Reuse, recycling & recovery enables access to affordable food, warmth & shelter amongst disadvantaged
Self-organising groups increase recycling, reuse & recovery activities
Recycling sites, reusing/recycling infrastructure enables city to adapt to new demand

circular systems. Data useful for urban metabolism monitoring have been collected in only a few cities (e.g., Paris and Amsterdam), and interpretation issues exist due to a lack of common conventions.[70,71] Most urban metabolism studies use highly aggregated data, which provide only a snapshot of resource or energy use, but no information about location, activities or people.[72]

There is a high data requirement for monitoring resource flows, a lack of follow-up and evaluation of the evolution of a city's urban metabolism, and difficulties in identifying the cause-and-effect relationships of the metabolic flows.[73] It is important that data spatially mapping metropolitan resource flows and ecosystem services are developed as a decision-making tool for politicians and policymakers. Tools that map the benefits and disbenefits of implementing a circular bioeconomic system will help to engage communities in decision-making processes and assist in the negotiations needed to resolve cross-boundary issues.[74]

4.11 ENGAGING LOCAL STAKEHOLDERS IN METRO-PLANNING

Stakeholder engagement in the planning and implementation of the circular bioeconomy is important if it is to be effective. However, in the context of weakly institutionalised, metropolitan planning, such forms of participation are typically not available.[75] Strategic, issue-based participation in metropolitan planning, with citizens coalescing around issues that are meaningful to them (e.g., managing waste, employment, energy and food security), may help to overcome this problem. It could also provide the opportunity for citizens to volunteer to engage in the co-provision of the new socio-technical systems required. This approach was used to develop Paris's Circular Economy Plan. It engaged a myriad of local actors (from civil society, industry, business, charities and government) from across the metro-region who not only contributed to the development of the CE plan but also were eventually involved in its implementation.[76]

4.12 CONCLUSIONS

There are sound ecological, social and economic reasons for implementing circular bioeconomic systems in metro-regions. These reasons are likely to become more pressing as global ecosystems degrade, the climate changes and resources become scarcer. There are international examples of where attempts are being made in practice to do this. However, current policy frameworks and institutions do not adequately support the approach. Consequently, there are many challenges to implementation. Nevertheless, the solutions presented here suggest it could be possible. Ideally, institutions responsible for the delivery of the circular bioeconomy at a metropolitan scale are needed to address the current lack of institutional capacity to develop strategic plans, policy and implement circular bioeconomic systems at this scale. These institutions would also require the competencies and resources to leverage such a transformation. Metropolitan plans for resource and ecosystem service management should be developed that provide clear guidelines for future development. These plans should encourage synergies between looping, regenerative and adaptive actions. Local stakeholders should be engaged in its creation. This collaborative approach will help to build local support for the circular bioeconomy, as well as build capacity in the system to enable successful implementation. Evidenced-based decision-making will be essential for the creation of optimal solutions as well as to engage public and political support in the implementation process.

Practitioner's perspective

Creating regenerative, circular systems at a regional scale is critical to reconnecting human and economic systems with the rest of nature. Currently, we do not have the policies or the tools in place to create circularity. This paper clearly identifies the cross-boundary issues that have hampered the delivery of regenerative systems. I have experienced some of those in practice. One relates to difficulties in coordinating policies, policy levers and resources across administrative boundaries, particularly in planning at the regional scale which engages with community actions. In addition, regenerative circular strategies might conflict with incumbent strategies already operating at different scales. Finally, the lack of useful data to inform decision-makers hampers the joined-up approach, which maximises local potential, needed to create regenerative systems.

Systems-thinking and joined-up action are very different from the linear thinking that has resulted in current policy frameworks and mindsets, which have precipitated the climate and ecological crisis. To create regenerative systems, we must move away from this reductionist thinking. We have created siloes of information and we overfocus on measurement and management, which leads to a paralysis of analysis. To move toward regenerative circular systems, we need to allow information to flow. We must enable actors to collaborate on "shared outcomes" across traditional siloes in sectors, organisations and their departments.

Pooran Desai *OBE is an environmentalist and entrepreneur, founder of OnePlanet, a company providing a digital platform enabling individuals or organisations to identify the potentials for interconnectedness and joined-up actions.*

NOTES

1 World Wide Fund for Nature (WWF) (2012) *Living Planet Report*. https://files.worldwildlife.org/wwfcmsprod/files/Publication/file/5bd0cghy29_Living_Planet_Report_2012_Biodiversity__biocapacity_and_better_choices.pdf

2 Camaren P and Swilling M (2012) *Sustainable Resource Efficient Cities: Making it Happen*. Nairobi: United Nations Environment Programme (UNEP).

3 Richter B D, Abell D, Bacha E, Brauman K, Calos S, Cohn A and Siegfried E (2013) Tapped out: How can cities secure their water future? *Water Policy*, 15(3): 335–363. https://doi.org/10.2166/wp.2013.105

4 International Energy Agency (IEA) (2008) *World Energy Outlook 2008*.

5 Klaus V H and Kiehl K (2021) A conceptual framework for urban ecological restoration and rehabilitation. *Basic and Applied Ecology*, 52: 82–94. https://doi.org/10.1016/j.baae.2021.02.010

6 Paes L A B, Bezerra B S, Jugand D and Agudo F L (2024) Navigating challenges and opportunities in urban circular bioeconomy: A comprehensive review and future directions. *Environmental Development*, 101039. https://doi.org/10.1016/j.envdev.2024.101039

7 World Economic Forum (WEF) (2017) *Project MainStream — Urban Biocycles, System Innovative on Environmental and Natural Resource Security*, 6. https://www3.weforum.org/docs/WEF_Project_MainStream_Urban_Biocycles_2017.pdf

8 Urban Agenda Partnership on Circular Economy (2019) *Survey Report on Regulatory Obstacles and Drivers for Boosting a Sustainable and Circular Urban Biobased Economy*. European Commission. https://futurium.ec.europa.eu/en/urban-agenda/circular-economy/library/survey-report-regulatory-obstacles-and-drivers-boosting-sustainable-and-circular-urban-biobased

9 Urban Agenda Partnership on Circular Economy (2019), see Reference 8.

10 Yang N-H N and Yang A (2022) Urban bioeconomy: Uncovering its components, impacts and the urban bio-symbiosis. *Cleaner Production Letters*, 3: 100015. https://doi.org/10.1016/J.CLPL.2022.100015

11 European Commission (2018) *A Sustainable Bioeconomy for Europe: Strengthening the Connection between Economy, Society and the Environment. Updated Bioeconomy Strategy. 2018*. https://eur-lex.europa.eu/legal-content/EN/TXT/?uri=CELEX%3A52018DC0673

12 Artioli F, Acuto M and McArthur J (2017) The water–energy–food nexus: An integration agenda and implications for urban governance. *Political Geography*, 61: 215–223. https://doi.org/10.1016/j.polgeo.2017.08.009

13 Artioli et al. (2017), see Reference 12.

14 Grossauer F and Stoeglehner G (2023) Bioeconomy — A systematic literature review on spatial aspects and a call for a new research agenda. *Land*, 12(1): 234. https://doi.org/10.3390/land12010234

15 Grossauer and Stoeglehner (2023), see Reference 14.

16 The food–water–energy nexus literature focuses on the interlinkages between these three systems. It investigates how to maximise the synergies between these systems to increase food, water and energy security through systems design, infrastructural solutions and resource management.

17 Artioli et al. (2017), see Reference 12.

18 Artioli et al. (2017), see Reference 12.

19 Grossauer F and Stoeglehner G (2020) Bioeconomy — Spatial requirements for sustainable development. *Sustainability*, 12(5): 1877. https://doi.org/10.3390/su12051877

20 Williams J (2023) Circular cities: Planning for circular development in European cities. *European Planning Studies*, 2(31): 14–35. https://doi.org/10.1080/09654313.2022.2060707

21 Grossauer and Stoeglehner (2023), see Reference 14.

22 Williams (2023), see Reference 20.

23 Schneider P, Meyer A and Plat K (2020) Potential of bioeconomy in urban green infrastructure. *Bioeconomy for Sustainable Development* 251–76. https://doi.org/10.1007/978-981-13-9431-7_13

24 Grossauer and Stoeglehner (2023), see Reference 14.

25 Williams J (2021) *Circular Cities: A Revolution in Urban Sustainability*. Routledge. https://doi.org/10.4324/9780429490613

26 Williams J (2022) Challenges to implementing circular development — Lessons from London. *International Journal of Urban Sustainable Development*, 14(1): 287–303. https://doi.org/10.1080/19463138.2022.2103822

27 Paes et al. (2024), see Reference 6.

28 Williams (2023), see Reference 20.

29 Paes et al. (2024), see Reference 6.

30 Grossauer and Stoeglehner (2023), see Reference 14.

31 Williams (2023), see Reference 20.

32 Grossauer and Stoeglehner (2023), see Reference 14.

33 Williams (2021), see Reference 25.

34 Knieling J, Jacuniak-Suda M and Obersteg A (2017) Urban–rural partnerships and governance of peri-urban areas in a European perspective. Towards regenerative regions. In A Colucci, M Magoni and S Menoni (eds.), *Peri-Urban Areas and Food–Energy–Water Nexus: Sustainability and Resilience Strategies in the Age of Climate Change*, pp. 31–37. Cham: Springer. https://doi.org/10.1007/978-3-319-41022-7_4

35 Deckmyn S (2018) Circular Flanders: Adaptive policy for a circular economy. In H Lehmann (ed.), *Factor X: Challenges, Implementation Strategies and Examples for a Sustainable Use of Natural Resources*, pp. 335–346. Cham: Springer. https://doi.org/10.1007/978-3-319-50079-9_23

36 Verga G C and Khan A Z (2022) Space matters: Barriers and enablers for embedding urban circularity practices in the Brussels Capital Region. *Frontiers in Built Environment*, 8. https://www.frontiersin.org/articles/10.3389/fbuil.2022.810049

37 Williams (2021), see Reference 25.

38 Williams (2021), see Reference 25.

39 See https://www.powertoprotein.eu/.

40 Williams (2021), see Reference 25.

41 Williams (2021), see Reference 25.

42 See https://www.parisculteurs.paris/en/home/.

43 Williams (2021), see Reference 25.
44 Williams (2021), see Reference 25.
45 Williams (2021), see Reference 25.
46 Williams J (2012) *Zero-Carbon Homes: A Road Map*. London: Routledge. https://www.routledge.com/Zero-carbon-Homes-A-Road-Map/Williams/p/book/9781849712491
47 Brick K (2008) Barriers for implementation of the environmental load profile and other LCA-based tools (Doctoral dissertation, KTH).
48 Williams (2023), see Reference 20.
49 Williams (2021), see Reference 25.
50 Williams (2023), see Reference 20.
51 Williams (2021), see Reference 25.
52 Williams (2021), see Reference 25.
53 Williams (2022), see Reference 26.
54 Brick (2008), see Reference 47.
55 Williams (2021), see Reference 25.
56 Knieling et al. (2017), see Reference 34.
57 Weldegebriel S K and Yeshitela K (2021) Measuring the semi-century ecosystem-service value variation in Mekelle city region, Northern Ethiopia. *Sustainability*, 13(18): 1–28. https://doi.org/10.3390/su131810015
58 Knieling et al. (2017), see Reference 34.
59 Williams (2021), see Reference 25.
60 Bastein A G T M, Verstraeten-Jochemsen J N, Rietveld E, Hauck M, Frijters E, Klijn O and Driessen B (2016, June 5) *Circular Amsterdam, A Vision and Action Agenda for the City and Metropolitan Area*. https://resolver.tno.nl/uuid:f7d0eaf1-8625-4439-ae8e-2168bfc20e95
61 Williams (2021), see Reference 25.
62 Williams (2021), see Reference 25.
63 Williams J (2021) Circular cities: What are the benefits of circular development? *Sustainability*, 13(10): 5725.
64 Allwinkle S and Cruickshank P (2011) Creating smart-er cities: An overview. *Journal of Urban Technology*, 18(2): 1–16. https://doi.org/10.1080/10630732.2011.601103
65 Allwinkle and Cruickshank (2011), see Reference 64.
66 Iacovidou E and Purnell P (2016) Mining the physical infrastructure: Opportunities, barriers and interventions in promoting structural components reuse. *Science of The Total Environment*, 557–558: 791–807. https://doi.org/10.1016/j.scitotenv.2016.03.098
67 Weldegebriel and Yeshitela (2021), see Reference 57.
68 McPhearson T, Pickett S T A, Grimm N B, Niemelä J, Alberti M, Elmqvist T, Weber C, Haase D, Breuste J and Qureshi S (2016) Advancing urban ecology toward a science of cities. *BioScience*. 66(3): 198–212. https://doi.org/10.1093/biosci/biw002
69 Williams (2021), see Reference 63.

70 Browne D, O'Regan B and Moles R (2009) Assessment of total urban metabolism and metabolic inefficiency in an Irish city-region. *Waste Management*, 29(10): 2765–2771. https://doi.org/10.1016/j.wasman.2009.05.008

71 Zhang Y (2013) Urban metabolism: A review of research methodologies. *Environmental Pollution*, 178: 463–473. https://doi.org/10.1016/j.envpol.2013.03.052

72 Browne et al. (2009), see Reference 70.

73 Pincetl S, Bunje P and Holmes T (2012) An expanded urban metabolism method: Toward a systems approach for assessing urban energy processes and causes. *Landscape and Urban Planning*, 107(3): 193–202. https://doi.org/10.1016/j.landurbplan.2012.06.006

74 Shahrokni H, Lazarevic D and Brandt N (2015) Smart urban metabolism: Towards a real-time understanding of the energy and material flows of a city and its citizens. *Journal of Urban Technology*, 22(1): 65–86. https://doi.org/10.1080/10630732.2014.954899

75 Häkli J, Kallio K P and Ruokolainen O (2020) A missing citizen? Issue based citizenship in city-regional planning. *International Journal of Urban and Regional Research*, 44(5): 876–893. https://doi.org/10.1111/1468-2427.12841

76 Williams (2021), see Reference 25.

5. Assessing circular economy transitions

Marcin Dąbrowski and Alexander Wandl

Keywords: circular economy; transitions; assessment; evaluation; holistic approach

Waste processing site in Łódzkie region, Poland. *Source*: Marcin Dąbrowski

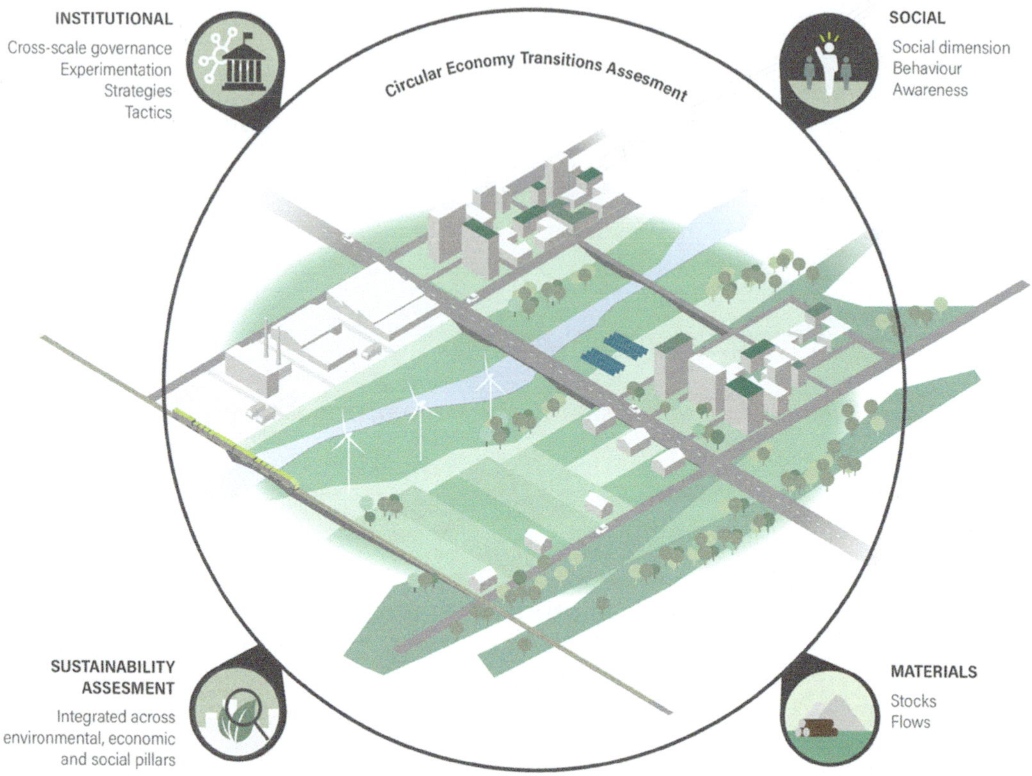

Source: Authors; graphic design by Fábio Alzate Martinez (TU Delft)

https://doi.org/10.1080/2578711X.2024.2418234

Key message

There is a gap between the lofty ambitions of new circular policies put forward by cities and regions and the actual messiness of the transition processes. This makes the question of monitoring and availability of data to support it all the more difficult and urgent.

5.1 OVERVIEW

To push forward a transition towards a clean, zero-waste circular economy (CE), cities and regions need to embed circularity goals and principles into their policies and urban planning. Succeeding in this effort requires developing tools for assessing the progress towards CE and to inform the relevant policies through effective evaluation. The current assessment methods face challenges in integrating the relevant dimensions and lack adequate data. Notably, spatial, governance and social aspects of CE transitions are often overlooked. In this chapter, we draw upon the academic literature and real-world policy examples to evaluate critically the existing approaches to CE assessment. Based on this, we provide recommendations to enhance the assessment of CE transitions in cities and regions.

5.2 THE CHALLENGE OF ASSESSING THE STATE OF CIRCULAR ECONOMY TRANSITIONS

In the wake of the deepening climate crisis,[1] the projected growth of material use[2] and the alarming pace of depletion of planetary resources,[3],[4] cities and regions across the world are rolling out CE policies and strategies. These often echo the circularity policy agendas put forward by central governments or supranational authorities, such as the European Union. In the private sector and civil society, there is also a surge in bottom-up experimentation and eco-innovations based on CE principles. To support circular transitions and capitalise on this momentum, we must assess their state effectively and identify ways to accelerate them while building the capabilities of cities and regions that drive these changes. Given the fuzziness of the concept of CE, making it prone to diverse interpretations by decision-makers,[5] its relative novelty and its implications for far reaching changes in socio-economic systems, there is neither consensus nor clarity on how to achieve this.

New assessment approaches are needed for multiple reasons. We need them to monitor the impacts of CE activities not only in terms of material stocks and flows and waste generation, but also, for instance, on the innovation performance of companies, on citizen awareness of circularity and their behaviour, or on the changes in the built environment. CE principles are enthusiastically and uncritically embraced by urban and regional policymakers across many countries, but in practice linear thinking about resource management still predominates. This results in the use of a CE approach to continue a "business-as-usual" approach to economic systems by improving resource efficiency, sticking to the growth perspective and failing to reduce consumption of resources. While in the realm of regional and urban policies and planning, this is reflected in the persistence of wasteful and unsustainable approaches to spatial development that result in the continuing urban expansion and growing resources use in cities and regions.

Thus, measuring how the actual sustainability and circularity of activities labelled as "zero waste" and based on CE principles is essential for devising evidence-based and effective policies and strategies to catalyse transitions away from the linear economic model of growth and spatial development. We also need to develop metrics to identify the extent to which the necessary conditions for enabling the CE transitions in cities and regions are in place. Moreover, monitoring and assessment of CE transitions is a valuable tool for communicating, disseminating and awareness-building among the diverse CE stakeholders, whose support is critical to anchor and mainstream CE. Such assessment is also essential for comparing the performance of CE policies across different places to enable lesson-learning. Finally, there is a strong demand for policy knowledge on CE, given that we lack "templates" for operationalising this concept at different territorial levels and considering the uncertainty about the performance of circular policy tools and approaches.

There is a gap between the lofty ambitions of new circular policies put forward by cities and regions and the actual messiness of the transition processes. This makes the question of monitoring and availability of data to support it all the more difficult and urgent,[6,7] calling for a flexible approach to the assessment of CE policies on the ground, mixing quantitative and qualitative indicators that cover a broad range of economic, social and environmental impacts, as well as the factors enabling or hindering transitions in an urban or regional context. However, at this early stage of transitions towards circular futures, there are still multifaceted barriers for promoting the application of CE principles.[8,9] These barriers should also be the object of evaluation, to identify and seek ways to overcome them.

In this chapter we provide an overview of what is currently done and proposed to address this need. We review the literature and a selection of examples of CE assessment frameworks used by local and regional government. We then identify some critical gaps in these approaches and develop a series of policy recommendations.

5.3 INSIGHTS FROM RESEARCH

The scholarly literature on the assessment of CE has exploded in the last few years, responding to the growing demand for such tools in the world of policy practice. In the limited space of this chapter, we provide a brief overview of this work.[10,11,12]

The existing assessment frameworks for CE focus on different levels, from micro (individuals, products, companies), meso (regions, industrial areas, cities) to macro (e.g., nation-states). They tend mostly to use methods such as life cycle assessment (LCA) to analyse the environmental impacts of products, services or other solutions; or material flow analysis (MFA) to quantify flows and stocks of materials in systems with specific boundaries, such as a country or a city.[13] These often sit alongside a plethora of other indicators that attempt to measure the wider impacts of CE actions, for instance, on well-being, job creation, innovation, etc. The current approaches to assessment vary greatly and lack a shared perspective on what needs to be measured.[14] The lack of consensus on terminologies and definitions among scholars, politicians and practitioners is one of the most important factors that limits the viability and usefulness of the current CE assessment and monitoring frameworks.[15] Most of the approaches rely on the most readily available waste data[16] and environmental indicators (e.g., recycling rates, CO_2 emissions), although social indicators (e.g., circular jobs, training opportunities), economic ones (e.g., household savings by reducing waste, local government spending on CE projects) and those related to digitalisation and the smart city are also considered.[17] The Organisation for Economic Co-operation and Development (OECD) gathered an overview of 474 CE indicators used by a range of cities and regions.[18] The review showed that environmental indicators predominated (39%), followed by those focused on governance (34%), economic performance (14%), and infrastructure and technology (8%). It also showed a lack of attention to the social and spatial dimensions: only 5% of indicators were concerned with jobs. Indicators related to the built environment correspond to 7% of the indicators studied. However, land-use indicators (e.g., new area development based on circularity principles) are very scarce (< 1%).

Another challenge is the difficulty in capturing cross-level interdependencies in terms of impacts of circular strategies. There are suitable tools for the assessment on specific levels. One example is the already mature LCA widely used to assess the performance of products and services at the micro-level or even industrial symbiosis systems at the meso-level. Another one is MFA, mostly used at the macro-level. But the existing metrics and frameworks hardly allow for grasping the interdependencies across developments at micro-, meso- and macro-levels (one exception being the Flemish approach[19]). Consequently, we lack understanding of how policy interventions at one level could affect those at another.[20]

What is also problematic is the narrow perspective on CE. Most of the current assessment frameworks consider flows of materials, but ignore their stocks,[21] for instance, those embedded in buildings or infrastructure and potentially available for "mining" and reuse. Most also focus mainly on material preservation strategies, such as recycling,[22] rather than on the use of materials.[23] These are some of the most basic circular actions and less desirable than those that aim to preserve the function the product (e.g., sharing) or preserve the product itself by extending its lifespan (e.g., reuse, repair). This is an important omission because

Table 5.1 The R-Ladder

Circular economy	Smarter creation and use of products	R0 Refuse	Turning a product redundant by cancelling its function, or by substituting it with a radically different product
		R1 Rethink	Intensifying product use (e.g., via product sharing or multifunctional products)
		R2 Reduce	More efficient use and/or manufacture of products using fewer natural resources and materials
Moving up the ladder entails consuming fewer natural resources and reducing environmental pressure	Extending the lifespan of products and parts	R3 Reuse	Reuse of discarded-yet-still-usable product, for the same purpose, by a different user
		R4 Repair	Repair and maintenance of broken or malfunctioning product to enable continuation of its original function
		R5 Refurbish	Refurbishing and/or modernising an older product so that the improved version can be used in the product's original function
		R6 Remanufacture	Using parts of a discarded product in a new product of the same function
		R7 Repurpose	Using discarded products or their parts in new products with a different function
	Useful application of materials	R8 Recycle	Processing of materials to achieve the original high quality or reduce to low quality
		R9 Recover	Incineration of materials, recovering their energy
Linear economy	Wasteful resource management	Landfill	Waste stored in landfill, to be avoided in CE

Source: Adapted from Potting et al. (2018)[24]

rethinking the ways in which materials and products are used is an important aspect of CE, corresponding to the higher level and, hence, more sustainable circular strategies on the so-called R-Ladder (Table 5.1).[25]

A practical weakness of the existing assessment frameworks is the limited availability of data. This is a major challenge for operationalising the assessment frameworks[26,27] and comparing performance between places, given the substantial differences in what data (on waste, flows and stocks of materials) are collected at different geographical scales across countries. As a result, we lack the means for sound measurement of the progress towards CE and the impacts of circular actions. This, in turn, creates a risk of pursuit of "circularity for circularity's sake".[28]

We also lack an integrated perspective on sustainability in the current CE metrics. Integrating the assessment of environmental, social and economic factors into one framework is a major methodological and technical challenge.[29,30] This also reflects the diverse and often narrow understandings of CE, limited only to material recirculation, while neglecting the wider systemic changes needed to reduce overconsumption of resources and use of CE policies as a driver for sustainable development[31] and overlooking the social dimension.[32,33]

Finally, reflecting the limited consideration of spatial factors for the deployment of circular strategies and of impacts of CE on spatial development in the current research and in policy practice (see chapters 1 and 4), the current assessment frameworks also tend to lack a place-based perspective. Most ignore the fact that the feasibility and impacts of strategies for closing material loops and reducing consumption of resources largely depend on the spatial conditions within the regional or local built environment. This limits the usefulness of the current assessment frameworks for cities and regions (see also chapter 2).

Some scholars propose frameworks that attempt to address these shortcomings. Cavaleiro de Ferreira and Fuso-Nerini[34] put forward a city- or regional-level framework for tracking the development of CE with a broad range of indicators, including demographics, policy environment and even aspects of the built environment. A regional assessment framework was proposed by Silvestri and colleagues[35] combining socio-health, economic and environmental indicators to measure the state of play of implementation of CE in regions. Meanwhile, Avdiushchenko[36] developed one that also integrated spatial and cultural factors. Likewise, for the macro-level assessment, Momete[37] proposed a framework blending a small selection of social, economic and environmental indicators, whereas Taelman et al.[38] proposed an assessment methodology for waste management that includes multi-size, multi-scale perspective as well as social and spatial indicators. Finally, Tonini and colleagues[39] operationalised a framework for household food waste management in the Amsterdam Metropolitan Area, demonstrating its feasibility, but also underscoring the high data intensity that this approach requires.

Overall, even though these frameworks represent steps in the right direction, they still suffer from the problems related to availability of data. In many cases, one could challenge the generic nature and relevance of some of the indicators used for CE assessment, making them unable to effectively capture the impacts of CE policies in specific territories and inform the development of capacities needed to implement them.

5.4 STATE OF PLAY IN POLICY PRACTICE

In the world of policy practice, multiple new frameworks for assessing CE have also been put forward. Here we review examples of macro-level frameworks from the European Union and the Netherlands. Then, looking below the national scale, we summarise some leading examples of assessment frameworks focusing on regional and urban levels. The coverage of the different components of these frameworks is summarised in Table 5.2.

5.4.1 European Union

The European Union has been leading the way in promoting CE transitions, with its CE Action Plan[40] being part of the European Green Deal. To assess progress toward its goals by its member states, a macro-level monitoring framework[41] has been developed. It not only focuses on waste generation (indicators on the amounts of different types of waste generated per capita), material consumption (resource productivity, material footprint), waste management (recycling rates per waste type), and secondary raw materials (e.g., circular material use rate, export and import of recycled materials), but also considers data on competitiveness and innovation in the CE sectors. The framework also includes the impacts of CE on sustainability performance (e.g., consumption footprint, emissions generated by production) and resilience (e.g., material import dependency). While being comprehensive on environmental and economic dimensions of sustainability, the framework overlooks the impacts from the social perspective and fails to monitor development of policies and governance conditions for CE transitions, especially at the subnational level. The framework can also be criticised for focusing on recycling mainly, while ignoring reuse or sharing activities to limit material consumption and waste generation.[42]

5.4.2 The Netherlands

The Netherlands has been at the forefront in setting ambitious national CE goals, which required the development of an adequate monitoring framework. The Dutch monitoring framework[43] includes a focus on flows, with indicators for (1) the input of materials to the national economy; then for (2) the use of materials through actions undertaken by diverse actors, and finally for (3) loss, that is, the waste created in the process. The framework distinguishes itself by employing the already mentioned R-Ladder.[44,45] In addition, the framework includes means for measuring the impacts of circular actions on the environment (with indicators on greenhouse gas emissions, biodiversity, toxicity of land and water, land use, water use, etc.) and socio-economic impacts (in terms of jobs, human health or supply risks) in the Netherlands and beyond (e.g., by monitoring the amount of waste exported for processing to third countries).

This is complemented by an assessment of the elements needed to support the transition towards CE, further informing policy. The indicators for the transition policy include, for instance, the number of companies that implement a circularity strategy as a business activity, development of knowledge on CE and its diffusion (e.g., number of scientific publications on CE), and provision of financial resources by the government to support circular

Table 5.2. Overview of the components of the monitoring frameworks reviewed

	Level	Flows of materials	Stocks of materials	(Re)use and waste avoidance (beyond recycling)	Environmental dimension	Economic dimension	Social dimension	Governance	Spatial dimension
European Union	National	+	–	+	+	+	–	–	–
The Netherlands (PBL)	National	+	–	+	+	+	+	+	±
Organisation for Economic Co-operation and Development (OECD)	Regional and urban	–	–	–	–	–	–	+	±
Flanders, Belgium	Regional	+	+	+	+	+	+	–	+
Amsterdam, the Netherlands	Urban	+	–	±	±	–	+	–	±

Note: *A "+" indicates that a given dimension is considered in the assessment, a "–" indicates that a given dimension is not considered, and a "±" indicates that a given dimension is partially considered.*

Source: *Authors.*

innovations and business assets. It also includes the readiness to embrace circular products by consumers and their declared behaviour with respect to sharing products, buying second hand, extending the lifetime of products or reduction of consumption. Other means of supporting the transition — such as the government's efforts to ensure coordination between the different actors, promote acceptance of circular products and services, or the use of different policy measures — are assessed qualitatively. While being very comprehensive, the framework misses an assessment of stocks of materials within the economy and a deeper consideration of space and the built environment, which would require focusing on the subnational scale.

5.4.3 Organisation for Economic Co-operation and Development (OECD)

In response to the major regulatory, knowledge or capacity barriers for implementation of CE policies in cities and regions, the OECD proposed[46] a framework for assessing the governance of CE for use by urban and regional-level authorities. The framework includes a checklist for actions on various aspects of policy (e.g., development of strategic visions, stakeholder engagement, capacity-building, data and assessment) through a simple scoreboard to assess progress towards them, tested in several European cities. It provides a helpful resource for governments wishing to assess progress towards establishing an enabling environment for promoting CE and covering a comprehensive range governance and policy aspects, including issues of awareness and stakeholder engagement. However, like most other frameworks, the OECD scoreboard considers spatial issues only to a very limited extent, advocating the facilitation of territorial linkages between urban and rural areas, and of neighbourhood-based CE initiatives.

5.4.4 Flanders, Belgium

The Flemish Circular Economy Monitor[47] is a leading of example of a regional assessment framework for CE. The monitor stands out by integrating macro-, meso- and micro-level perspectives across over 100 indicators. On the macro-level, covering the region of Flanders, the monitor considers inputs of materials to the economy (e.g., direct material input, domestic material consumption, water consumption), the circular actions that involve different "R-strategies" (Table 5.1) from recycling to reuse (e.g., household and industrial recycling of waste, reuse of goods per capita, circular material use), and the outflow that is the emissions and waste produced (e.g., CO_2 emissions, production of different types of waste). In this, the Flemish monitor resembles the Dutch monitoring framework. It also looks into the effects of the Flemish CE, considering not only material footprint but also ecological impacts (with indicators such as use of space, carbon footprint of consumption, soil contamination and remediation), and socio-economic impacts (e.g., employment

 https://doi.org/10.1080/2578711X.2024.2418234

and turnover in the CE). The Flemish monitor also includes the intermediate level, corresponding to four regional "need systems": housing, food and water, consumer goods, and mobility. This helps to understand the regional context in which CE unfolds and the needs to which it should respond. Finally, the monitor includes micro-level data on specific products and services related to CE, such as the turnover of repair shops for mobile phones or reuse of various types of goods via second-hand shops. This allows for a fine-grained perspective on the performance of CE.

Remarkably, the Flemish approach considers the stock of current raw material reserves needed for the construction sector (clay, sand, loam, etc.), while also providing insights into the spatial conditions for CE (with indicators on built-up areas and open spaces) and positive impacts within the built environment (e.g., lifespan of buildings, recycling rate of building materials, amount of rented social housing). It also attempts to measure the social impacts of CE, with a focus on well-being and health indicators, such as exposure to air pollution, water scarcity or homelessness. In conclusion, the Flemish monitor is an example of an integrated approach to the assessment of CE, cutting across economic, environmental and social dimensions of sustainability. It also attempts to include a spatial perspective to better understand the spatial conditions for CE development and its impacts within the built environment. What the monitor misses, however, is consideration of aspects of governance of the transition towards CE.

5.4.5 Amsterdam, the Netherlands

Amsterdam, one of the front-runners in development of urban CE policies, has adopted a distinctive approach to monitoring its circular transition[48] based on the "doughnut economics" concept.[49] The approach insists on reducing the footprint of the economy to fit within the ecological boundaries of the planet and avoid depleting its resources, while making sure that actions to achieve these goals are based on a sound social foundation.

Building on this idea, the Amsterdam Circular Monitor assesses five domains in Amsterdam and, where data are available, its metropolitan region. First, similarly to the other assessment frameworks described above, it focuses on the inputs to the economy, with indicators on the amounts of different types of materials, such as construction materials, food or consumer goods consumed in the city/region, together with emissions of CO_2 produced in the process. Second, it should include indicators with a focus on the micro-level to measure the ways in which materials are used by companies and consumers (e.g., duration of use, reuse practices). However, this dimension of the monitor remains in development due to the lack of adequate data. Third, the monitor considers outputs in terms of waste. It measures household waste collection by public authorities, assessing the amounts of separated waste corresponding to different types of materials (organic, plastics, construction waste). Fourth, it measures industrial waste collection and processing done by companies, with similar metrics on the amounts of waste produced per material type, with an assessment of the reusability of these materials. Finally, reflecting the principle of "doughnut economics", the monitor considers the general welfare of society. In this, it builds on the wider Dutch government's commitment to pursue and measure progress towards "broad prosperity", encompassing a range of domains, from the social (wealth inequality, health and mental well-being), through to qualities of the living environment (e.g., accessibility, quality and cost of housing), to indicators concerned with jobs (including circular jobs specifically) and income.

The monitor stands out by considering the materials consumed and waste produced in the built environment, and by the focus on the geographical dimension of flows of waste. Unlike other frameworks, Amsterdam's monitor, building on the sufficiently granular waste data available in the Netherlands, maps where waste is produced and processed (within/out the region), and provides valuable insights for designing place-based solutions and policies to promote CE at the regional scale, while also considering interdependencies with other places and the impacts of circular policies beyond the regional boundaries.

That said, the monitor cannot yet capture several important dimensions. It does not include indicators that consider spatial conditions for CE or its spatial impacts. It also lacks any indicators on governance. While being particularly ambitious on the evaluation of social impacts of CE, the monitor also misses the assessment of economic impacts and effects of CE activities on the environmental performance of the metropolitan region, beyond measuring the carbon footprint and material use. Finally, it does not yet allow for precise measurement of certain aspects it puts forward, but rather sets a direction for the development of new metrics for those. This concerns, in particular, indicators for the use of materials and the impacts of circular activities on specific aspects of "broad prosperity".

5.5 CONCLUSIONS: PRINCIPLES FOR AN INTEGRATED AND PLACE-BASED CIRCULAR ECONOMY ASSESSMENT

In sum, the examples covered in this chapter show there are shortcomings not only in the assessment of material flows but also in evaluating whether and how regions and cities steer the CE transition, how circular strategies are integrated across scales and sectors, and how sustainable they actually are. To start developing an integrative and cross-disciplinary monitoring framework, CE transition assessment should include at a minimum the following five dimensions: (1) the social dimension; (2) the material dimension; (3) an integrated sustainability assessment; (4) an institutional dimension; and (5) a built environment dimension, which is particularly relevant for cities and regions. Below, we provide a set of principles concerning each of these.

5.5.1 The social dimension

The social aspect of the CE is often overlooked (see chapter 3). We need assessment frameworks that consider factors such as creating circular jobs, providing opportunities for disadvantaged groups through circular activities, and enhancing quality of life, well-being, equity and health, even if it remains difficult to discern causal relations between circular activities and these domains. Furthermore, raising awareness is crucial for changing local social and behavioural patterns, which can be barriers to CE adoption. Enhanced awareness can reshape the habits of citizens, companies and the public sector, bridging the gap between policy goals and real-world implementation. The social assessment dimension should also encompass corporate awareness of circular practices, regional stakeholder awareness of circular policies, and the daily practices of citizens regarding waste, consumption and product/material reuse.

5.5.2 Material flows and stocks

Current material flow measurement approaches often lack the spatial precision required to unpack the "black box" of city or regional metabolism. We need to develop adequate metrics of flows and stocks of materials to track progress toward a CE and guide policy development.[50] To effectively map and evaluate waste and material flows for informed decision-making at different scales (national, regional, city), we must collect highly detailed data at the appropriate scale and standardise metrics across locations to enable comparisons and benchmarking.

5.5.3 Taking sustainability seriously

Assessment frameworks need to consider the environmental, social and economic impacts of material looping processes, which can entail unintended negative effects. Examples include high-energy use in recycling stations; increasing transport needs for the collection of reusable products generating additional emissions; negative externalities of circular activities (e.g., odours, noise); or negative health impacts for workers involved in extracting valuable materials from waste.

One option to address this is to better align LCA with the more comprehensive United Nations Sustainable Development Goal (SDG) indicators. We propose the use of an integrated sustainability assessment of circular activities that underscores the interconnectedness between the different SDGs and the importance of connecting social, economic, and ecological systems for gauging whether and how CE can contribute to sustainable development Moreover, stakeholder involvement is critical to collect the right data, co-decide on the goals and scope of the assessment, or even for the identification, selection and development of suitable indicators.

5.5.4 Enabling an institutional environment

Few of the existing CE assessment frameworks consider the institutional environment needed to enable the transition towards circular cities and regions. Drawing inspiration from the transitions management framework,[51] we propose developing an assessment entailing four components of an enabling institutional environment for the circular transition. First, we need to assess the presence and performance of strategic-level activities aimed at the long term. Examples include visioning, goal-setting and elaboration of long-term transition strategies together with stakeholders. Second, we should consider the tactical transition actions that target the mid-term changes in established structures, institutions, regulations, and physical or financial infrastructures (e.g., incentives for circular business models, circular public procurement, conditionalities for area development). Third, assessment should focus on taking stock of, and the presence of, measures for supporting (local) experimentation and short-term actions through which alternative circular practices are practiced, tried out and showcased. Lastly, it is equally important to assess the presence and quality of activities aimed at collective learning and sharing knowledge about the ongoing circular transition. This is needed to cope with uncertainties related to making CE work and helps to inform policy development and raise awareness and capacity among the stakeholders.

5.5.5 The built environment

CE does not happen in a vacuum but is literally "taking place" in specific territories and spatial configurations, taking advantage of existing infrastructures. Thus, assessment needs to consider the state and transformation of the built environment and the related construction sector. Where does a city or region stand on implementing biobased and other circular construction methods? Is it still experimental or mainstream? Are circular practices considered in new construction or in urban regeneration projects? We also need to assess how the built environment is supporting other sectors to become more circular. The transition towards circularity will entail a spatial reorganisation and relocation of economic activities from global to regional and local levels (see chapter 2). Are the spatial structures and land available to house these new (re-)manufacturing activities and their externalities, as well as different logistical challenges? Are the spatial planning regulations fit to deal with the nuisances caused by circular activities, which may be dirty, smelly and loud? Does urban and regional policy consider keeping strategic spatial reserves and preserve industrial areas and infrastructures to host circular activities? Finally, where can CE activities be deployed to regenerate polluted and neglected areas, degraded through linear economic activities? Answering these critical questions will require developing new metrics, both quantitative and qualitative, and including them in a place-based CE assessment.

Practitioner's perspective

As a practitioner developing software that assists companies and governments in the transition from linear to CEs by finding optimal solutions for waste, I encounter many challenges with waste data. The European Waste Statistics collection, in particular, traditionally prioritises the negative environmental impact of waste. It is increasingly evident that this approach is based on outdated principles and falls short of addressing the accelerating resource depletion. To be able to track progress towards a CE, we must shift our perspective to waste, recognising it as a valuable resource rather than just a problem to be mitigated, as it was perceived two decades ago when waste statistics requirements were established.

A significant limitation is the current waste statistics reporting standard, which categorises waste primarily by hazard level. While this classification serves safety and regulatory purposes, it lacks a comprehensive understanding of the waste's potential as a secondary resource in circular activities. To harness the full potential of waste as a resource, we must delve deeper into its characteristics and origins.

In practice, we have observed increased interest from companies in understanding the ultimate fate of their waste and identifying secondary resource opportunities. However, at present, European Waste Statistics do not track waste beyond its environmental harm threshold. To fully unlock waste's potential as a resource, we must expand our tracking and reporting mechanisms to follow its journey to the final destination, going beyond recycling, reprocessing or reuse, and also report the creation of secondary products. We need to consider factors such as material composition, origin, treatment methods, usage history and reasons for generation. Such detailed data on waste not only would inform government-level decision-making but also foster innovative waste management solutions at the waste processor level.

***Rusnė Šilerytė** is co-founder and chief technical officer (CTO) at geoFluxus, a sustainability-driven technology start-up based in Rotterdam, the Netherlands*

NOTES

1 Intergovernmental Panel on Climate Change (IPCC) (2023) *Climate Change 2023: Synthesis Report. Contribution of Working Groups I, II and III to the Sixth Assessment Report of the Intergovernmental Panel on Climate Change*, core writing team: H. Lee and J. Romero (eds.). Geneva: IPCC. https://www.ipcc.ch/report/ar6/syr/

2 Organisation for Economic Co-operation and Development (OECD) (2019) *Global Material Resources Outlook to 2060: Economic Drivers and Environmental Consequences*. Paris: OECD. https://www.oecd.org/development/global-material-resources-outlook-to-2060-9789264307452-en.htm/

3 Circle Economy (2023) *The Circularity Gap Report 2023*. Amsterdam: Circle Economy. Amsterdam: Circle Economy. https://www.circularity-gap.world/2023

4 United Nations Environment Programme (UNEP) (2016) *Global Material Flows and Resource Productivity. An Assessment Study of the UNEP International Resource Panel.* H. Schandl and M. Fischer-Kowalski (eds.). Paris: UNEP. https://www.unep.org/resources/report/global-material-flows-and-resource-productivity-assessment-report-unep

5 Fratini C F, Georg S and Jørgensen M S (2019) Exploring circular economy imaginaries in European cities: A research agenda for the governance of urban sustainability transitions. *Journal of Cleaner Production*, 228: 974–989. https://doi.org/10.1016/j.jclepro.2019.04.193

6 European Commission (2022) *Circular Cities & Regions Initiative: Methodology for the Implementation of a Circular Economy at the Local and Regional Scale*. Luxembourg: Publications Office of the European Union. https://data.europa.eu/doi/10.2777/068045

7 Marin J, Alaerts L and Van Acker K (2020) A materials bank for circular Leuven: How to monitor "messy" circular city transition projects. *Sustainability*, 12(24): 10351. https://doi.org/10.3390/su122410351

8 Obersteg A, Arlati A, Acke A, Berruti G, Czapiewski K, Dąbrowski M, Heurkens E, Mezei C, Palestino M, Varjú V, Wójcik M and Knieling J (2019) Urban regions shifting to circular economy: understanding challenges for new ways of governance. *Urban Planning*, 4(3): 19–31. https://doi.org/10.17645/up.v4i3.2158

9 Organisation for Economic Co-operation and Development (OECD) (2020) *The Circular Economy in Cities and Regions: Synthesis Report*. https://www.oecd.org/regional/the-circular-economy-in-cities-and-regions-10ac6ae4-en.htm

10 For a more detailed review, see Moraga G, Huysveld S, Mathieux F, Blengini G A, Alaerts L, Van Acker K, De Meester S and Dewulf J (2019) Circular economy indicators: What do they measure? *Resources, Conservation and Recycling*, 146: 452–461. https://doi.org/10.1016/j.resconrec.2019.03.045

11 For a more detailed review, see Parchomenko A, Nelen D, Gillabel J and Rechberger H (2019) Measuring the circular economy – A multiple correspondence analysis of 63 metrics. *Journal of Cleaner Production*, 210: 200–216. https://doi.org/10.1016/j.jclepro.2018.10.357

12 For a more detailed review, see Saidani M, Yannou B, Leroy Y, Cluzel F and Kendall A (2019) A taxonomy of circular economy indicators. *Journal of Cleaner Production*, 207: 542–559. https://doi.org/10.1016/j.jclepro.2018.10.014

13 Walzberg J, Lonca G, Hanes R J, Eberle A L, Carpenter A and Heath G A (2021) Do we need a new sustainability assessment method for the circular economy? A critical literature review. *Frontiers in Sustainability*, 1. https://www.frontiersin.org/articles/10.3389/frsus.2020.620047

14 Bîrgovan A L, Lakatos E S, Szilagyi A, Cioca L I, Pacurariu R L, Ciobanu G and Rada E C (2022) How should we measure? A review of circular cities indicators. *International Journal of Environmental Research and Public Health*, 19(9): 5177. https://doi.org/10.3390/ijerph19095177

15 Sileryte R, Wandl A and van Timmeren A (2023) A bottom-up ontology-based approach to monitor circular economy: Aligning user expectations, tools, data and theory. *Journal of Industrial Ecology*, 27(2): 395–407. https://doi.org/10.1111/jiec.13350

16 Organisation for Economic Co-operation and Development (OECD) (2020) *The OECD Inventory of Circular Economy Indicators*. OECD. https://www.oecd-ilibrary.org/urban-rural-and-regional-development/the-circular-economy-in-cities-and-regions_10ac6ae4-en

17 Bîrgovan et al. (2022), see Reference 14.

18 OECD (2020), see Reference 16.

19 Alaerts L, Acker K V, Rousseau S, Jaeger S D, Moraga G, Meester S D, Van Passel S, Compernolle T, Bachus K, Vrancken K and Eyckmans J (2018) *Towards a Circular Economy Monitor for Flanders: A Conceptual Basis*. Brussels: Flemish Government. https://vlaanderen-circulair.be/src/Frontend/Files/userfiles/files/Towards%20a%20CE%20monitor%20for%20Flanders.pdf

20 Harris S, Martin M and Diener D (2021) Circularity for circularity's sake? Scoping review of assessment methods for environmental performance in the circular economy. *Sustainable Production and Consumption*. 26: 172–186. https://doi.org/10.1016/j.spc.2020.09.018

21 Harris et al. (2021), see Reference 20.

22 Moraga et al. (2019), see Reference 10.

23 Harris et al. (2021), see Reference 20.

24 Potting J, Hanemaaijer A, Delahaye R, Hoekstra R, Ganzevles J and Lijzen J (2018) *Circular Economy: What We Want to Know and Can Measure. Framework and Baseline Assessment for Monitoring the Progress of the Circular Economy in the Netherlands*. The Hague: PBL Netherlands Environmental Assessment Agency. https://www.cbs.nl/en-gb/publication/2018/03/circular-economy-what-we-want-to-know-and-can-measure.

25 The R-Ladder is based on a hierarchy for the preferred approaches to waste management put forward by Ad Lansink, a Dutch parliamentarian, as early as 1979, suggesting that incineration and landfill were the least desirable approaches, whereas the avoidance of waste generation and reuse were the most desirable. The approach was later picked up by the Dutch government and internationally as a reference and a basis to develop a hierarchy of CE strategies.

26 Harris et al. (2021), see Reference 20.

27 Potting J, Hekkert MP, Worrell E and Hanemaaijer A (2017) *Circular Economy: Measuring Innovation in the Product Chain*. Planbureau voor de Leefomgeving (PBL). https://dspace.library.uu.nl/handle/1874/358310

28 Harris et al. (2021), see Reference 20.

29 Saidani et al. (2019), see Reference 12.

30 Corona B, Shen L, Reike D, Rosales Carreón J and Worrell E (2019) Towards sustainable development through the circular economy — A review and critical assessment on current circularity metrics. *Resources, Conservation and Recycling*, 151: 104498. https://doi.org/10.1016/j.resconrec.2019.104498

31 Corona et al. (2019), see Reference 30.

32 Mies A and Gold S (2021) Mapping the social dimension of the circular economy. *Journal of Cleaner Production*, 321: 128960. https://doi.org/10.1016/j.jclepro.2021.128960

33 Schroeder P, Lemille A and Desmond P (2020) Making the circular economy work for human development. *Resources, Conservation and Recycling*, 156: 104686. https://doi.org/10.1016/j.resconrec.2020.104686

34 Cavaleiro De Ferreira A and Fuso-Nerini F (2019) A framework for implementing and tracking circular economy in cities: The case of Porto. *Sustainability*, 11(6): 1813. https://doi.org/10.3390/su11061813
35 Silvestri F, Spigarelli F and Tassinari M (2020) Regional development of circular economy in the European Union: A multidimensional analysis. *Journal of Cleaner Production*, 255: 120218. https://doi.org/10.1016/j.jclepro.2020.120218
36 Avdiushchenko A (2018) Toward a circular economy regional monitoring framework for European Regions: Conceptual approach. *Sustainability*, 10(12): 4398. https://doi.org/10.3390/su10124398
37 Momete D C (2020) A unified framework for assessing the readiness of European Union economies to migrate to a circular modelling. *Science of The Total Environment*, 718: 137375. https://doi.org/10.1016/j.scitotenv.2020.137375
38 Taelman S, Tonini D, Wandl A and Dewulf J (2018) A holistic sustainability framework for waste management in European cities: Concept development. *Sustainability*, 10(7): 2184. https://doi.org/10.3390/su10072184
39 Tonini D, Wandl A, Meister K, Unceta P M, Taelman S E, Sanjuan-Delmas D, Dewulf J and Huygens D (2020) Quantitative sustainability assessment of household food waste management in the Amsterdam metropolitan area. *Resources, Conservation and Recycling*, 160: 104854. https://doi.org/10.1016/j.resconrec.2020.104854
40 European Commission (2020) *A New Circular Economy Action Plan for a Cleaner and More Competitive Europe*. https://eur-lex.europa.eu/legal-content/EN/TXT/?qid=1583933814386&uri=COM:2020:98:FIN
41 European Commission (n.d.) *Circular Economy Monitoring Framework*. https://ec.europa.eu/eurostat/cache/scoreboards/circular-economy/
42 European Commission (2022), see Reference 6.
43 Planbureau voor de Leefomgeving (PBL) (2023) *Integral Circular Economy Report 2023. Assessment for the Netherlands*. https://www.pbl.nl/sites/default/files/downloads/2023-pbl_integral-circular-economy-report-2023-assessment-for-the-netherlands_5109_0.pdf
44 Potting et al. (2018), see Reference 25.
45 Potting et al. (2017), see Reference 27.
46 OECD (2020), see Reference 9.
47 Flemish Government (2023) *Circular Economy Monitor*. https://cemonitor.be/en/home-english/
48 Municipality of Amsterdam (2020) *Amsterdam Circular Monitor*. Gemeente Amsterdam. https://assets.amsterdam.nl/publish/pages/867635/amsterdam_circular_monitor.pdf
49 Raworth K (2017) *Doughnut Economics: Seven Ways to Think like a 21st-Century Economist*. Chelsea, VT: Chelsea Green.
50 Sileryte R, Sabbe A, Bouzas V, Meister K, Wandl A and van Timmeren A (2022) European Waste Statistics data for a circular economy monitor: Opportunities and limitations from the Amsterdam Metropolitan Region. *Journal of Cleaner Production*, 358: 131767. https://doi.org/10.1016/j.jclepro.2022.131767
51 Loorbach D, Wittmayer J M, Shiroyama H, Fujino J and Mizuguchi S (eds.) (2016) *Governance of Urban Sustainability Transitions: European and Asian Experiences*. Tokyo: Springer Japan. http://link.springer.com/10.1007/978-4-431-55426-4

6. Policy recommendations for facilitating an urban and regional circular economy

Karel Van den Berghe, Marcin Dąbrowski, Ellen Van Bueren and Joanna Williams

Keywords: urban planning; spatial planning; circular cities; circular regions

Waste processing site in Hamburg. *Source*: Marcin Dąbrowski

SCALE	RECOMMENDATIONS
International 	1 - Promote the development of standardised approaches to collecting data on waste, material flows and stocks at the national and regional levels 2 - Embrace an integral approach to evaluating the impacts of circular economy initiatives 3 - Invest in research and development of new metrics to capture the social, environmental, economic and spatial dimensions and impacts of circular economy at different levels 4 - Invest in the development of capacity for steering and informing circular economy transitions
National 	1 - Set ambitious circular economy transition agendas and foster a cross-sectoral dialogue ato engage the big economic and societal players at the national scale 2 - Incentivise the adoption of circular principles by sub-national governments, companies and citizens through regulation, taxation, finance, and other policy tools 3 - Use circular economy as a strategic backbone for integration of goals and actions across the relevant national policies 4 - Develop national strategies to limit resource consumption 5 - Propose spatial visions and strategies that embrace circular economy as an important factor for national spatial development
Regional / Local 	1 - Nurture territorially-embedded communities of practice to inform policy and spatial planning for circular economy transition 2 - Use interregional or international ciruclar economy knowledge co-creation and sharing platforms to learn and draw lessons 3 - Embrace a 'care-full' approach to circular activities, using them as a vector for social justice and inclusion 4 - Rethink and valorise interconnections across urban, peri-urban, rural areas through the prism of material flows to harness the regenerative potential of circular economy 5 - Strengthen capacities, resources and competences of the regional authorities to provide a strong institutional leadership needed to bring regional stakeholders together to promote the circular economy agenda within the new functional geographies shaped by material flows

Key message

A shift towards a circular city or a circular region entails developing a place-based and critical approach to CE policy that considers the often-overlooked social and political aspects of sustainability, going beyond the technical aspects of resource efficiency and waste management, and incorporates the principles of regeneration, resilience, and justice.

6.1 OVERVIEW

This closing chapter brings together the main messages from each chapter. It formulates a policy agenda for circular cities and regions. It does so by providing a set of recommendations for policy practice. These are addressed at authorities and policy stakeholders at the international, national and subnational levels.

6.2 THE MAIN MESSAGES OF THIS BOOK

The purpose of this book is to explore the concept of circular economy (CE) and its implications for cities and regions. CE is an alternative paradigm to the dominant linear model of production and consumption that aims to reduce waste, reuse resources and regenerate natural systems. It has gained increasing attention from policymakers, practitioners and researchers as a potential solution to the multiple challenges of environmental degradation, resource scarcity, social inequality and economic stagnation. However, CE is not a one-size-fits-all approach, but rather a context-specific and place-based process that requires a holistic and systemic perspective.

Therefore, this book offers a critical and comprehensive analysis of CE with an emphasis on the role of space for CE transition of cities and regions. Current CE policies emphasise closing material loops in industrial processes and economic activities. However, what is overlooked is that the operationalisation of these policies does happen in "space", at a specific set of locations within a particular urban or regional context, in relation to other locations connected by flows of materials. In other words, space enables, but also limits, to what extent the CE transition can be achieved. What is more, several potential benefits from territorialising CE policies could be reaped by cities and regions when adopting a more place-based and holistic perspective on the matter. These range from harnessing CE activities, to revamping the local or regional economy based on circular business models and innovations, to regenerating the degraded, neglected, and often peripheral areas and rethinking their relations to the core of the urban region, to improving the region's resilience to geopolitical shocks, or to creating new opportunities for citizens and promoting social justice.

Our definition of a circular city and region expands the techno-economic focus of the current approaches to CE in cities and regions and, instead, proposes a more holistic, spatial and relational

https://doi.org/10.1080/2578711X.2024.2418236

perspective, emphasising the embeddedness of networks of circular activities and flows of materials within specific spatial settings. Hereby, a shift towards a circular city or a circular region entails developing a place-based and critical approach to CE policy that considers the often-overlooked social and political aspects of sustainability, going beyond the technical aspects of resource efficiency and waste management, and incorporating the principles of regeneration, resilience and justice. Building on this point of departure, we then explored this spatial and relational perspective on the circular city and region by diving into four themes, covered by chapters 2–5 respectively: (1) CE as a geopolitical strategy; (2) a "care-full" CE; (3) circular bioeconomy in city-regions; and (4) assessing and monitoring circular transitions in cities and regions.

The main messages of this book are as follows:

- CE is a context-specific process ridden with complexity and uncertainty that requires a holistic and systemic perspective to design and implement adequate policies at the subnational level.
- An "all-hands-on-deck" approach is needed to integrate policies and actions vertically across levels of government and horizontally across sectors and administrative boundaries, to promote transversal learning, overcome the multiple barriers for CE implementation on the ground, and to harness the potential of circular innovations to drive sustainable urban and regional development.
- Cities and regions are key actors and arenas for the circular transition, as they can create new forms of connectivity, infrastructure, and sustainability within and beyond their boundaries. As such, it is at the urban and regional scales that we need to focus our efforts and invest in place-specific policies and strategies to experiment with, upscale and mainstream CE.
- CE can be part of a strategic response to the global resource depletion crisis, geopolitical turmoil and re-/deglobalisation trends by enhancing the regions' resilience and competitiveness by closing material loops within the regional scale and rendering regional economies less dependent on global value chains, which are increasingly prone to disruptions. Given the (implicit) cherry-picking of, in this case, Europe,[1] the "realistic" implementation of a CE can be a simultaneous solution for the decades-long lost battle against climate change, and the geopolitical dependence of materials, energy and products.
- CE offers opportunities to promote the social dimension of sustainability by fostering and integrating care-oriented relations and processes in proposed circular projects and policies.
- To support the governance of transition towards CE we need to develop new metrics and engage a broad range of stakeholders in a holistic assessment of progress towards transition goals to inform place-based circular policies.

6.3 POLICY RECOMMENDATIONS

Based on these findings, we suggest a range of policy recommendations to accelerate the CE transition and to harness its potential to boost environmental, economic and social sustainable development of cities and regions. We recognise that the CE transition entails cross-level interdependencies and will require multi-scalar policy efforts, but, for the sake of clarity, we categorised our recommendations according to three levels: international, national and regional. While our recommendations are biased towards the European perspective, many of them can also provide lessons and inspiration for policy change at the national and subnational levels beyond Europe.

6.3.1 International level

As explained in chapter 2, the current geopolitical turmoil that the European Union (EU) is facing can give a much-needed push to shift towards CE. If a narrow perspective on CE prevails (i.e., considering it solely a strategy to address unsustainable resource consumption and reduce environmental impacts by designing out waste), this new paradigm risks following a similar fate as many previous promising but fuzzy ideas that were very enthusiastically received, but then quickly fizzled out due to implementation challenges. This may happen if one remains stuck in seemingly endless debates on definitions and implementation conundrums, as may happen with the concept of sustainability,[2] eventually risking becoming a subject of political polarisation, harming its potential for operationalisation and mainstreaming. Given the numerous practical barriers, the difficulty in demonstrating tangible positive results of circularity so far, and the challenges in adoption of circular business models and policies that take the concept seriously, this is one possible scenario for the CE concept. That said, in the context of the war in Ukraine erupting in 2022 and contributing to an energy crisis in Europe, the EU formed policy answers to cope with this challenge surprisingly quickly. However, these emergency responses lack in many cases consideration for ecological and social aspects. This is where a window of opportunity opens for moving the EU towards CE that combines resilience and limits dependency, and built on ecological, economic, social and just principles. Though, at the same time, we do not advocate for a local CE in principle. As explained by North,[3] and the fifth CE principle explained in chapter 1, localism implies as local as possible. Thus, it does not exclude that in some cases other scales are relevant and other agendas, for example, trust and peace built upon trade relations (cf. the rationale of the EU), do not have importance.

Next, as discussed in chapter 5, the relevant international organisations, such as the EU, Organisation for Economic Co-operation and Development (OECD) or the United Nations's agencies, should promote the development of standardised approaches for collecting data on waste and on material flows and stocks states. Ideally, this should include data at the regional level, which would allow for not only cross-national but also cross-regional comparisons, benchmarking and monitoring of progress towards CE targets at those levels, while providing the regional and local governments with valuable data to design, implement and evaluate place-based CE policies. As we showed, measuring circular activities that go beyond recycling and consider the reuse of materials and goods or capturing the impacts of CE within a specific territory remain methodologically challenging (see chapter 5). This, in turn, points to the need for actors such as the EU especially — but also the national and subnational governments — to invest substantial resources in research and development of new metrics to capture the social, environmental, economic, and spatial dimensions and impacts of CE at different levels. Without this, we will lack the means to develop, track, evaluate and improve territorial CE policies. Development of adequate metrics is also critical for the (measurement of) success of the implementation of the European Green Deal, putting a strong emphasis on circularity, and for the mobilisation of EU Cohesion Policy funds to support actions accelerating CE transitions.

Another important policy lesson for the EU — but also to some degree for national governments in Europe and elsewhere — concerns the need to invest in the development of capacity for steering and informing CE transitions. This entails rethinking (multi-level) governance through the prism of material flows and their geography, which cuts across administrative and national boundaries. Moreover, the development of evidence-based policy for steering CE transition in cities and regions needs to be informed by integrated assessment tools able to track transition progress in specific territories. The EU should mobilise its existing tools for transnational and cross-regional knowledge transfer — such as Interreg, the European Circular Economy Stakeholder Platform or its transnational research programme Horizon Europe — to experiment with new governance approaches for place-based CE policy and build capacity to develop adequate assessment methods.

6.3.2 National level

The national level was not our central focus across the different chapters as currently much of the ongoing CE policy innovation happens at local and regional levels, while the geopolitical pressures strengthening the case for CE is foremost international — at least as seen from a European perspective. That being said, many CE policy documents that have been developed during last decade are national, and national governments have developed or are developing regulations, labels or policy tools for CE.

We argue that the importance of the national level for CE transition will probably increase in the short term. CE may be trapped in what we might call a "grey zone" between the levels of government. Local CE activities are difficult to scale up and move beyond the initial experimental phase. This may be because of a lack of perceived urgency of the CE agenda by the wider public, lack of regulations or lack of finance to move from experimentation to systemic change. Also, within the EU, national governments are mostly "waiting" for the EU level to show the way forward in terms of implementation and funding of CE policies.

Given the recent geopolitical developments disrupting global value chains, however, the pressure for national governments to translate the European Green Deal into effective policies will increase and CE could become a vehicle for pursuing an integral sustainability agenda and strengthening supply chain resilience. We argue that the national governments should strive to capture the urgency concerning CE emerging from the international level and help local and regional circular initiatives to flourish.

The national level — and this is true not only for EU member states but also for national governments in other parts of the world — can act as a catalyst and supporter of place-based CE policies of cities and regions. This can be achieved by setting ambitious CE transition agendas and fostering a cross-sectoral dialogue to engage the big economic and societal players at the national scale. Beyond this, central governments have the powers to incentivise the wider adoption of circular principles by subnational governments, companies and citizens through regulation, taxation, finance and other policy tools. They also have the capacity to connect the CE policy agenda to other sectoral policies of relevance, such as energy, climate or industrial policies. We recommend they use CE as a strategic backbone for the integration of goals and actions across the relevant national policies to address the polycrisis (climate, energy, housing, etc.) that the linear economy exacerbates.[4]

Given that cities and regions now operate far beyond the Earth's ecological capacity, we urgently need to move towards systems contained within those (planetary) boundaries. National governments need to provide actors with guidance on how much resources can be consumed to remain within the planet's carrying capacity. This, in turn, requires developing a bold and integrated approach to resource management based on national strategies to limit resource consumption to inform and steer sectoral policies and subnational planning policies (see chapter 4). As part of such an approach, national governments should also consider introducing regulatory tools to improve resource efficiency, for instance, through caps on national resource consumption. Introducing such measures would require treading carefully, though, anticipating the possible backlash against them and the uneven socio-spatial distribution of economic burdens they would entail. In summary, we need strong governmental intervention, backed by a persuasive narrative on circular futures, to radically shake up the current economic model and anchor CE principles firmly on the policy agenda.

Finally, most national governments (unlike supranational organisations such as the EU) have powers and competences in spatial planning. We made a strong case for considering the spatial conditions that can accommodate or hinder circular activities and the spatial implications of these activities. We argue that national governments should develop spatial visions and strategies that embrace CE as an important factor for the national spatial development. This will provide a frame of reference, guidance and tools for deployment of spatial CE policies and strategies at the subnational level.

6.3.3 Regional and local levels

Last but not least, we offer a set of recommendations for cities and regions, which — as we argued in this book — are probably the most important policy actors in the CE transitions.

As explained in chapter 2, currently the operationalisation of CE, on the one hand, scaling-up from the local practical operationalisation (cf. product and built environment) and, on the other, downscaling from the global international policy level, is converging at the urban or regional level. It is not a question of (concrete) "design" or of (abstract) "policy", but both.[5] Therefore, we made a case for a more spatial and localised perspective on CE by highlighting the current local to regional characteristics of many CE initiatives and by stressing the need to consider the spatial aspects and networks of CE, which are determined by the patterns, socio-economic networks and relations, and ecological systems being part of urban and regional spatial development. Steering those through spatial planning policies is one of the core functions and competences of local and regional governments. In addition, municipal and regional governments are critical for CE transitions because they can combine the roles of: (1) promoters of CE among private and civic actors through the provision of information, goals and targets; (2) facilitators of connections and dialogue among the stakeholders and levels of government; and (3) enablers of circular transitions by providing regulations, resources and incentives for the relevant local and regional stakeholders to embrace the CE.[6]

While we applaud the efforts that cities and regions are making to support CE activities, we stress the need to keep on innovating and to consider more thoroughly the spatial and socio-economic aspects of CE. For this, cities and regions need to adopt a co-creative approach to gain insights and learn from the perspectives of diverse stakeholders from across disciplines, economic sectors, institutional and administrative boundaries. In the face of complexity and uncertainty related with CE, local and regional officials often lack the capacity and insights to develop evidence and place-based CE policies on their own. Instead, they should seek to nurture territorially embedded communities of practice to tap into a broader pool of knowledge, resources, and actor networks to inform policy and spatial planning for CE. At the same time, we strongly recommend that subnational governments engage in the currently burgeoning interregional or international CE knowledge co-creation and sharing platforms to enable lesson-drawing from experiences of other places.

Moreover, municipal governments in particular should embrace a "care-full" approach to circular activities. This approach can help synergise the positive social and environmental impacts of CE projects and policies within different communities, especially the most vulnerable and marginalised ones (see chapter 3). This promising aspect of CE is currently neglected and municipalities, acting locally and being the closest to the citizens, are best positioned to integrate this approach into place-specific policies, spatial plans and strategies to promote CE. Otherwise, the risk is creating CE "winners and losers', with the most economically disadvantaged disproportionally in the latter camp, leading to further fostering of social and political divisions.

Finally, regional governments play an especially important role in promoting a shift towards CE by connecting diverse activities in the different areas composing a region, from the urban

 https://doi.org/10.1080/2578711X.2024.2418236

cores to the fringes, from peri-urban to rural areas, through hard and soft regional infrastructures. Networks of circular activities, related to extraction, transporting, processing and consumption of materials, are embedded within regional patchworks of those spaces. Regional or metropolitan authorities are able to shape and influence the interrelations between those places and to develop spatial strategies at the regional scale. We recommend that regional policymakers and planners rethink those interrelations through the prism of CE and, especially, its regenerative potential (see chapter 4) and interdependencies related to flows of materials across the regional space. This, in turn, requires developing capacities, resources and competences of the regional authorities to provide a strong institutional leadership needed to bring regional stakeholders together around the CE agenda and working with new functional geographies shaped by waste and material flows that cut across diverse regional spaces and across administrative divisions.

7 IN CLOSING

We hope these policy recommendations will help policymakers, practitioners, researchers and citizens to advance the CE transition in cities and regions in Europe and beyond. We also hope this book inspires further research on CE from different disciplines and perspectives, especially on the under-researched spatial, geographical, social and even political dimensions of circularity. We strongly believe that CE is not only a technical and economic challenge, but also a social and political opportunity to create more sustainable futures for cities, regions, Europe and the world.

Practitioner's perspective

There is a noticeable shift from a linear to a circular approach to economic and spatial development in cities and regions. While ambitious policy goals are set, the implementation of circular policies often falters, though. Technologically, we are continuously making scientific discoveries, and companies are capable of innovating, but the practical application of these innovations and implementation of urban and regional policies to support them often faces challenges related to existing laws and regulations. For example, the Dutch building code (Bouwbesluit) does not force builders to build with a circularity principle, while the spatial planning law (Omgevingswet) does not explicitly require adopting circular principles in spatial development. Rethinking laws to enable circular innovations is thus critical for delivering effective circular policies.

The City of Amsterdam, along with its partners, has developed a knowledge platform called CIRCULAW (https://www.circulaw.nl) to help governmental actors make better use of regulations to promote CE by mapping out the existing laws and regulatory instruments across levels of government. This allows for identifying legal gaps that matter for circularity at different levels, for clarifying the responsibilities of the different actors within specific material flows, and for promoting vertical collaboration among the different governmental actors. CIRCULAW also seeks to promote structural collaboration with the national government to establish a feedback loop between law development and enforcement. This, in turn, provides a basis with which to formulate concrete suggestions for new legislation, giving the subnational authorities more agency in shaping an enabling environment for circularity.

CIRCULAW keeps evolving and developing, particularly in areas such as timber construction. The goal is to reinforce cooperation on regulations to support circularity at all levels of government, initially nationally and eventually internationally. After all, we are all working towards the same circular objectives.

Joost van Faassen *is a Strategic Urban Designer for the Municipality of Amsterdam*

NOTES

1 Cf. Latour B (2022) Is Europe's soil changing beneath our feet? *Géopolitique, Réseau, Énergie, Environnement, Nature*, 2: 92–97. https://geopolitique.eu/en/articles/is-europes-soil-changing-beneath-our-feet/

2 van Bueren E and De Jong J (2007) Establishing sustainability: Policy successes and failures. *Building Research & Information*, 35(5): 543–556. https://doi.org/10.1080/09613210701203874

3 North P (2010) Eco-localisation as a progressive response to peak oil and climate change – A sympathetic critique. *Geoforum*, 41(4): 585–594. https://doi.org/10.1016/j.geoforum.2009.04.013

4 Cf. Tooze A (2022) *Welcome to the World of the Polycrisis*. Financial Times. https://www.ft.com/content/498398e7-11b1-494b-9cd3-6d669dc3de33

5 Cf. Van den Berghe K and Vos M (2019) Circular area design or circular area functioning? A discourse-institutional analysis of circular area developments in Amsterdam and Utrecht, The Netherlands. *Sustainability*, 11(18): 4875. https://www.mdpi.com/2071-1050/11/18/4875

6 Organisation for Economic Co-operation and Development (OECD) (2020) *The Circular Economy in Cities and Regions*. Paris: OECD. https://doi.org/10.1787/10ac6ae4-en

For Product Safety Concerns and Information please contact our EU representative GPSR@taylorandfrancis.com Taylor & Francis Verlag GmbH, Kaufingerstraße 24, 80331 München, Germany

Batch number: 10745903

Printed by Printforce, the Netherlands